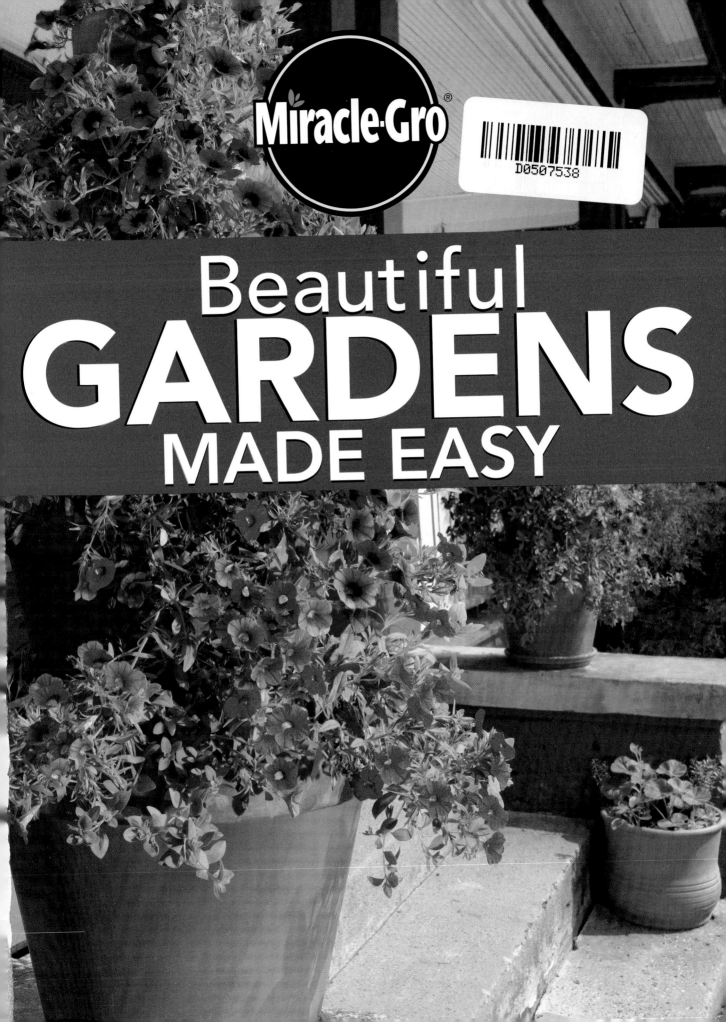

Miracle-Gro®

D0507538

Beautiful
GARDENS
MADE EASY

For more than 50 years Miracle-Gro has been the name America comes to for gardening success, and the reason is simple: We believe anyone can achieve joy, wonder, and satisfaction by the simple act of growing something and bringing beauty into the world. We're proud to bring you our first book, based on the vision that glorious gardens—and great gardeners—grow out of a series of small, easy projects. This book is full of beautiful ideas for every part of the yard and guides you to achieve them instantly and successfully. We hope you will discover more joy, wonder, and satisfaction in gardening each and every day.

Contents

FOREWORD BY PETER STRAUSS **6**

HOW TO USE THIS BOOK **8**

29

GARDENS THAT WELCOME **10**
Quick solutions for entryways and other first impressions.

Garden ideas in this chapter: Instant Doorstep Garden; Curbside Flowers Overnight; Rose Arbor Romance; Backdoor Makeover; Front Porch Seasonals; Garden Gate Upgrade

GARDENS THAT ENCLOSE **36**
Easy ways to create privacy and intimacy outdoors.

Garden ideas in this chapter: No-Dig Hedge; Front Porch Privacy; Instant Backyard Getaway; Bower of Flowers; A Cool, Misty Glade

GARDENS THAT TRANSFORM **58**
Pure garden magic that turns flaws into assets instantly.

Garden ideas in this chapter: Make a Tight Space Seem Bigger; Disguise and Distract; Light for a Dark Area; Hide the Air-Conditioner; Water Garden Magic

GARDENS THAT DISPLAY **80**
Designer shortcuts for showing off favorite plants and garden objects.

Garden ideas in this chapter: Violets in the Kitchen; Sculpture in the Garden; Framing a View Through a Side Yard; Hang Your Garden on a Wall; Small-Space Solution: Go Vertical; Easy Orchid Window Garden; Growing Cut Flowers Indoors

50

68

106

GARDENS THAT ENTERTAIN 110
Smart ways to create sociable outdoor areas in a single afternoon.

Garden ideas in this chapter: Living Herb Centerpieces; Light Up Your Party; From Potting Bench to Party Bar; Double-Duty Six-Packs; Think Big When Staging a Party

GARDENS THAT PRODUCE 132
Small projects for a big harvest of vegetables, fruits, herbs, and cut flowers.

Garden ideas in this chapter: Small-Space Vegetable Beds; A Privacy Screen That Produces; Portable Cut-Flower Garden; Grow Your Own Oranges, Lemons, and Limes; Hanging Herbs; Lettuce for Beauty and Bounty

GARDENS THAT SUPPORT 158
Clever ideas for backstage growing, holding, and storage facilities that make gardening fun— and that look good too.

Garden ideas in this chapter: Storage That Shines; A Beautiful Home Nursery; Instant Holding Beds with Wattle; Dressing Up a Potting Bench; Building a Cold Frame

112

143

168

HARDINESS ZONE AND FROST MAPS 180

RESOURCES 182

GENERAL INDEX 183

INDEX OF FEATURED PLANTS 190

INDEX OF TECHNIQUES 191

CREDITS 192

Foreword by Peter Strauss

Actor Peter Strauss, in his garden next to a fountain he designed, is the spokesperson for Miracle-Gro owing to his lifelong personal interest in gardening. "I'm a fanatic," he freely admits. He gardens on 10 acres outside of Santa Monica—next to a 30-acre citrus orchard with 3,006 orange trees that he works himself.

This is the first time I've had the pleasure of working on a book. Best of all, it happens to be about gardening, my favorite pastime and joy. In fact this is the first time that the promise of the Miracle-Gro brand has been extended to a book, one designed to help every gardener succeed at having a bigger, better, more colorful, and healthy garden with terrific results. The projects inside are designed to be easy and fun to achieve. All great gardens and gardeners begin with small successful projects, and *Beautiful Gardens Made Easy* has been created to provide you with the guidance and support to accomplish your goals.

For one thing the book is full of neat ideas such as the project on portable

Peter Strauss was catapulted onto the pop culture stage by the role he played in a 1976 TV miniseries. Today he philosophizes that his true calling is as a gardener—one who loves all plants.

cut flower gardens on page 142. I just planted a cutting garden for my wife, but I never thought I could grow one in containers.

How about the project for growing your own citrus trees (page 146) in pots? I maintain a citrus orchard of 30 acres, and when the trees are all in bloom, the fragrance is beyond belief. So it makes me happy to know that anyone with the inclination can enjoy the intoxicating perfume of fresh orange blossoms.

Or how about the project for growing succulents vertically on a wall like a work of art (page 94)— what a fun idea! I happen to love succulents—they were the first plants that caught my attention after I graduated from college and moved to Southern California. A plant show of exotic cacti and succulents got me started, and before long I had 300 plants in pots on my apartment roof. So here's an extra tip from me: Watch

out for those plants you might take a liking to. Before you know it you might turn into a plant and gardening fanatic like me!

Another feature of the book I really like is the straight-on presentation of basic techniques. Even weeding can be made less of a chore (see page 27). In fact the featured techniques that accompany each project cover practically everything— they're almost a course in basic gardening. Don't miss page 191 for a helpful index to the techniques.

On the same pages with the techniques you'll find gardening tips from me. I've been gardening for more than 30 years. It gives me great pleasure to share cuttings—and advice. I've learned a lot, some of it the hard way. I hope you'll find my tips useful and sometimes amusing.

This book conveys a lot of the challenge and fun of gardening that I've discovered over the years. It is a

joy to nurture living things, to express yourself creatively and artistically while also exploring the worlds of biology and botany.

Let's face it—gardening is about making the world around us beautiful and celebrating plants. I don't think I have ever met a plant I didn't like or didn't learn to appreciate. In fact I'm obsessed with my garden. I typically start out early in the morning thinking I'll only garden a few hours and the next thing I notice is the sun setting! Gardening grounds me and gives me so many rewards—a stately oak tree, a juicy tomato, a rose. It provides rewarding exercise and concentration and ultimately a feeling of accomplishment and a state of bliss. Where else but a garden can you get all that? And here's one more tip: Carry out even a few of the easy projects in this book and before you know it you'll be surrounded by beautiful gardens that welcome or enclose or transform or display or entertain or produce. *Beautiful Gardens Made Easy* will guide you so like me, you can discover the absolute joy and satisfaction of gardening!

◄ Whether weeding, watering, fertilizing, deadheading—or simply enjoying his cactus and succulent collection (a lifelong obsession)—Peter Strauss says the activity of gardening renews his spirit, filling him with joy, hope, and happiness. "At the end of the day I'd rather be a gardener than participate in almost any other activity you can name."

How to Use This Book

This book is designed to teach you about plants and gardening techniques while developing projects that will immediately enhance your quality of life.

Sunny or shady, wet or dry, hot or cold, inside your home or outdoors—no matter where you'd like to grow a beautiful plant or a garden— you'll find inspiration, practical ideas, and down-to-earth instructions in the pages of this book.

Start with any project that appeals to you—each one will have a big impact on the beauty and pleasure you see and feel in your garden or in your home. If it's winter, check out the projects beginning on page 80, in particular "Violets in the Kitchen," "Easy Orchid Window Garden," and "Growing Cut Flowers Indoors."

Another place to find projects for inclement weather is in "Gardens That Support," beginning on page 158. Here you'll find solutions for getting all your gardening gear organized and setting up efficient work spaces for timely plantings.

"Gardens That Welcome," which begins on page 10, may well be your first stop. This is because at the front door is often the single best place to begin focusing your gardening efforts. Landscaping a whole property can be a daunting prospect and unthinkably expensive if done all at once. Instead, concentrate your efforts on one beauty spot at a time and the impact will be greater. You'll also be able to enjoy the work and never feel overwhelmed or underfunded.

Each project is paired with a fundamental gardening technique and a unique group of plants—195 of the best plants are profiled and illustrated—so that as you complete the projects, you will also become a better gardener.

The projects have been designed to be installed in a matter of hours, or at most in a weekend. And nearly everything shown in this book is readily available at your local home and garden center.

Project Ideas:
The project ideas are simple, fast, and designed for every part of the yard. Each project is designed to fill a particular need, such as to make the entrance to your home more beautiful or to give an attractive view from the house, such as what you see while standing at the kitchen sink.

Details Count:
Each project has photos of little details that make a big difference in achieving a successful effect.

Shopping Lists:
Each project has two shopping lists, one for materials and equipment, one for the plants you'll need to achieve the effect shown in the photograph.

Before Photos:
Most of the projects have a before photo so you can see the transformation that is possible with a simple, easy, well-thought-out gardening project.

After Photos:
The beauty shots taken after the planting show finished results.

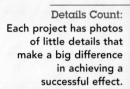

Instant Doorstep Garden

Plant Focus:
Each project is accompanied by a focus on a particular group of plants that suits the project's scope, and goals.

Basic Techniques:
Each project is accompanied by a fundamental gardening technique. Build on these and be a better gardener.

Plant Profiles:
Descriptions of important plant groups help you customize the projects to suit your needs—feel free to substitute! In many cases a key plant recommended for the project is highlighted.

Technique Details:
The techniques are sometimes shown in detail photos, but often in step-by-step photos to make the way as easy and clear as possible.

Peter Strauss Tips:
On the techniques pages, Peter Strauss shares his practical insights about gardening, based on his own experiences.

Fragrance for Containers

Choosing the Right Pot

Plant Portraits:
The plants represent an ideal of their type and give a visual clue to help you when shopping or planning your garden. Labels with the scientific name of the species or cultivar of the plant allow you to be very accurate when requesting the plant at your home and garden center or nursery.

Instructions:
Follow the instructions, usually step-by-step, and they will help you grow to be an expert.

In this chapter

12 INSTANT DOORSTEP GARDEN
Create a welcoming container garden
at the front door—in minutes!

14 Plants: Fragrance for Containers
15 Technique: Choosing the Right Pot

16 CURBSIDE FLOWERS OVERNIGHT
Make an all-season flower bed next to the driveway
in a single afternoon.

18 Plants: Bedding Plant All-Stars
19 Technique: Making a No-Dig Bed

20 ROSE ARBOR ROMANCE
Grace your entry walk with the beauty and fragrance of
a rose-covered arbor.

22 Plants: Great Climbing Roses
23 Technique: Planting a Bare-Root Rose

24 BACKDOOR MAKEOVER
Energize the rear family entry
with a garden worth coming home to.

26 Plants: Tropicals Outdoors
27 Technique: Preventing Weeds

28 FRONT PORCH SEASONALS
Stage an ever-changing welcome with drop-in
container plants.

30 Plants: Seasonal Drop-Ins for Container Gardens
31 Technique: Choosing the Right Soil for Containers

32 GARDEN GATE UPGRADE
Give your gateway a welcome mat paving of colorful wine
bottles and fragrant creeping thyme.

34 Plants: Fragrance Underfoot
35 Technique: Choosing and Applying Plant Food

welcome

Gardens That Welcome

Front yards and front doors that open their arms wide to say "Welcome!" have a miraculous, uplifting effect on everyone who sees them, from visitors, neighbors, and passersby to you and your family. Whether you're moving into a new house or updating a home you've lived in for a while, small beautification projects along the driveway, in front of the garage, at the front and back doors, and in the front yard add up to big first impressions.

Instant Doorstep Garden

When you move into a new house, get acquainted with the yard and what's there before you visit a local nursery. Concentrating on one garden spot at a time produces quick results that make you feel satisfied and proud.

▲ Hidden Utility Pot
If you have no time to transplant from the grower's plastic pot to clay, use a slightly larger clay pot as an instant slipcover.

▲Finishing Touch
To keep potting soil from splashing onto leaves and flowers, carpet the surface with a layer or two—up to 1 inch—of sandstone pebbles or river gravel.

▲A Drain Hole for Every Pot
As a basic rule, pots used outdoors should have one or more drain holes. If needed, use a power drill.

Starting a new garden at the front door often makes sense. After all, you see it every time you come and go, and watering and gardening make you feel at home in your new neighborhood.

This front door garden (opposite) was completed in a few hours, using actively growing plants already in full bloom and fully developed tree-form standards.

To keep specimen plants in top form throughout the growing season, be vigilant about watering daily (sometimes twice in the heat of summer). Feed regularly to keep flowering plants covered with blooms and foliage types looking luxuriant. Regular grooming to remove dead flowers and shriveled leaves improves performance.

An important tradition of gardening for pleasure is to plant for fragrance and pleasant scents along walks, up steps, over arches, and next to windows. Here, fragrant petunias and everblooming jasmine, along with a variety of rose- and lemon-scented geraniums, do the job.

Materials and Equipment

- Two 14" clay pots
- Ten 12" clay pots
- Eight 10" clay pots
- Four 6" clay pots
- Two large bags premium potting mix
- One 25-pound bag river gravel
- 6 yards chain and 2 hooks for hanging baskets
- Jute twine
- Watering can
- Pruning shears
- All-purpose, water-soluble plant food

The Plants
shown on the opposite page

- Two 12" blue mini petunias in hanging baskets
- Two tree-form standard variegated rose geraniums
- Twelve 4" blue lobelias
- Two tree-form standard coleus
- One 10" pink petunia
- Six 6" scented geraniums
- Four 10" pink calibrachoas
- Two 10" yellow calibrachoas
- One 8" 'Maid of Orleans' jasmine
- Two 6" fancy-leaved geraniums
- Two 10" English ivies

Plan of Action

1 Position clay pots on steps.
2 Add plants, starting with the largest. Remove plastic growing pots; set plant in clay pot and fill in all around with potting soil.
3 Plant six of the lobelias around the base of each tree-form rose geranium.
4 Install hooks for hanging baskets; replace original hangers with metal chains 36 inches long (or to other length to suit the site).
5 Water as needed to keep all roots moist; apply all-purpose, water-soluble plant food weekly according to label directions.

BEFORE

Mass for effect is the idea behind this doorstep garden. Before, the steps were bare, and the house might have appeared vacant had it not been for the two urns with ferns. Now the steps are home to a collection of scented geraniums, fragrant petunias, jasmine, and colorful coleus. The original black door was painted a warm gray in harmony with the steps.

Fragrance for Containers

A HELIOTROPE is a frost-tender perennial that grows like an annual bedding geranium. The fragrance is soft; some noses smell cherry pie. It blooms from spring until fall frosts.

B 'STARGAZER' ORIENTAL LILY grows from a bulb; plant 4 inches deep in spring for richly perfumed flowers on 24-inch stems several weeks in early to midsummer. Hardy in Zones 5–8.

C 'INGRID BERGMAN' ROSE, a hybrid tea, is a strong plant with disease-resistant, dark green leaves. The velvety flowers give off a light, clean fragrance that is the essential old rose. Hardy in Zones 6–10.

D 'BLUE JACKET' DUTCH HYACINTH grows well in pots, or you can set the bulbs to root in glasses of water for late winter or spring blooms that are intensely fragrant. Hardy in Zones 3–7.

E CANDLESTICK FLOWERING TOBACCO is a hardy annual that grows from a tiny seed in spring to a majestic 6-foot-tall plant by the end of summer. The tubular flowers smell richly of jasmine, especially in the evening.

FRAGRANT FLOWERS AND SCENTED LEAVES are essential parts of what makes a garden a place where you want to be. Certain flowers and leaves are so strongly associated with their fragrance that the mere mention of their names conjures up how they smell: rose, lilac, lily, rosemary, and lavender, to name some all-time favorites.

Let your nose be the judge of which fragrant plants you'd like to grow. Not all roses are fragrant, nor are all mockoranges, honeysuckles, or jasmines. Even among the so-called scented geraniums, some, 'Old Scarlet Unique' for example, are pungent at best. Chrysanthemums have a surprisingly sweet astringent smell that seems to go perfectly with the fall season.

A balance of sweet and savory smells pleases most noses—for example, pairings such as jasmine and lavender, or a rose such as 'Double Delight' with apple or nutmeg geranium.

Helliotropium 'Marine'

Lilium 'Stargazer'

Rosa 'Ingrid Bergman'

Hyacinthus orientalis 'Blue Jacket'

Nicotiana sylvestris

Choosing the Right Pot

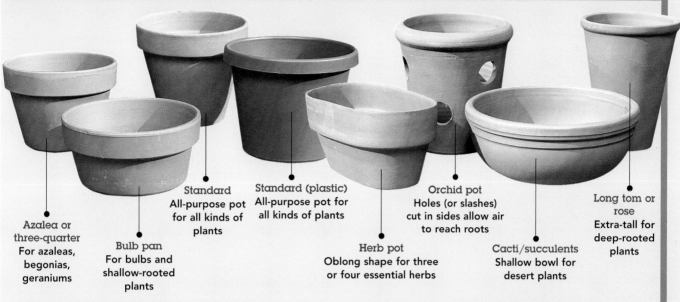

Azalea or three-quarter
For azaleas, begonias, geraniums

Bulb pan
For bulbs and shallow-rooted plants

Standard
All-purpose pot for all kinds of plants

Standard (plastic)
All-purpose pot for all kinds of plants

Herb pot
Oblong shape for three or four essential herbs

Orchid pot
Holes (or slashes) cut in sides allow air to reach roots

Cacti/succulents
Shallow bowl for desert plants

Long tom or rose
Extra-tall for deep-rooted plants

▲ Clay or plastic? The only plastic pot is the one identified as such in the center above. Decorative and utility growing pots come in all sizes and many different colors. Pots for outdoors often need to be bigger than you think. The larger the pot in a given situation, the more stable, the less likely to tip over, the less likely to dry out between waterings, and the less likely to overheat. In general, it is better to have fewer, larger pots rather than many little ones scattered about.

Having a supply of clean pots on hand is the mark of a good gardener. Unglazed clay pots come in three basic styles. The standard is as high as it is wide across the top and can be used for growing most plants. The three-quarter, also called an azalea pot, is three-fourths as high as it is wide. As the name suggests, it is good for azaleas and other shallow-rooted plants, such as begonias and bedding geraniums. The bulb pan is shorter than it is wide; it is a good choice for potting spring bulbs in fall to force into early bloom indoors.

You'll also find clay-colored plastic pots. The main difference, besides weight, is that moisture transpires through an unglazed clay pot. This has both a cooling and a drying effect, which means roots will be cooler but you'll have to water more. To stabilize against wind, see "Stabilizing" (page 25).

You can buy most any type of clay pot in faux, or artificial, materials, such as plastic or foam. Such materials have two advantages over clay: They are lightweight—a big plus for large pots, which can be very heavy when filled with soil—and they resist damage from freezing when left outdoors on cold winter days.

◀ 'Purple Wave' petunias, lime coleus, and scented geraniums in plastic pots make a simple and upbeat step garden.

"SOAK CLAY POTS
overnight in a pail or tub of fresh water before you plant in them. That way the porous, unglazed clay or terra-cotta won't sap moisture from the soil."

—Peter Strauss

BEFORE

An ordinary intersection of driveway, sidewalk, and lawn turns into a colorful, charming entrance with the simple addition of a raised bed packed with flowers. Built and planted on top of the lawn in a single afternoon, the bed also directs traffic to the driveway and sidewalk in a way that puts the home's best face forward. Such plantings require little work to maintain.

SPRING

SUMMER

FALL

Curbside Flowers Overnight

A raised, no-dig bed, planted for season-to-season beauty, adds instant appeal to a front yard. Even better, it requires only a pleasurable amount of upkeep to thrive.

▲ Dreaming of Spring
Plant groups of daffodil bulbs in fall for spring color; they bloom year after year.

This inviting design makes an attractive accent next to the driveway and sidewalk where characterless concrete and turf previously converged. The newfound beauty is sure to boost your spirits and that of your visitors and neighbors.

The 12-inch-deep raised bed, shaped by a bottomless 5-foot-square cedar frame, sits on top of the once-bare turf. The ideal home for annuals, perennials, and bulbs holds a mix of topsoil and garden soil that drains excess moisture easily. Topping it off, the frame's ledge offers a place to sit while puttering. Once planted, the bed requires little maintenance other than feeding and watering.

The planting scheme shown here was installed in fall to put on a good show into winter, when a deep freeze wipes out the ornamental kale and lays the perennial mums and ornamental grass to rest until spring. The return of warm weather awakens the perennials and triggers the daffodils and cold-hardy pansies to bloom. You must replace kale each year or substitute it with another bedding or perennial plant.

Build the frame (instructions are on page 19) using weather-resistant cedar lumber, which gradually grays. Or apply stain or paint in the color you desire.

▲ Try Different Arrangements
Set potted plants in place, then move them around until the layout pleases you.

Materials and Equipment

- Four 10' 2×6s (cut eight, 58" long)
- Two 10' 2×4s (cut four, 60" long)
- Two 8' 2×4s (cut sixteen, 11" long)
- Two 8' 2×2s (cut eight, 17" long; cut eight, 11" long)
- Two 1-pound boxes of 3" galvanized or stainless-steel screws
- Cordless drill with phillips bit
- Shovel and wheelbarrow
- Fourteen 40-pound bags topsoil
- Fifteen 1-cubic-foot bags garden soil

The Plants
shown on the opposite page

- Bulbs: 48 daffodils; 48 tulips; 100 grape hyacinths (Muscari)
- One 8" ornamental grass
- Four 6" ornamental kale
- Four 6" chrysanthemums
- Four six-packs of blue-purple pansies
- Four six-packs of white pansies
- Four 'Happy Returns' daylilies

▲ Pansies and Bulbs Together
Pansies planted over bulbs help disguise the bulbs' dying foliage in late spring.

Plan of Action

1 Choose a 5-foot-square site for the raised bed. Mow grass as short as possible.
2 Select lumber at a home center or building supplier; have pieces cut to length.
3 Assemble precut lumber and secure with screws (see photos page 19).
4 Fill the bottom of the planter with topsoil. Add the garden soil and mix the soils.
5 Plant the bulbs first; finish with annuals and perennials.

▲ Frost-Resistant Beauty
Ornamental kale and mums add captivating textures to the fall garden.

Bedding Plant All-Stars

A PANSIES are big grown-up annual cousins of the perky Johnny-jump-up violas. Both do best in cooler weather. They need evenly moist, well-drained soil and protection from hot direct sun through midday.

B GERANIUMS of the annual bedding type are not true geraniums but rather *Pelargonium* hybrids. They prosper in breezy, dry places and look their best when dead flowers are routinely removed. Good drainage and regular applications of all-purpose plant food are essential.

C PETUNIAS are annuals that come in most colors and can be upright mounds or cascading. You'll also find mini petunias and a related annual called *Calibrachoa*. They need moist soil, sun, and regular applications of all-purpose plant food.

D IMPATIENS are annuals that come in jewel colors that make them the most popular choice for flowers in the shade. In cool weather they tolerate sun, as do the New Guinea hybrids, which also come with boldly variegated leaves.

E COLEUS are warm-weather annuals grown for colorful leaves, which can be deeply cut, frilled, and ruffled. With moist, well-drained soil and regular applications of all-purpose plant food, they grow well in both sun and shade.

If you like the idea of an easy-care garden with season-to-season good looks, you can depend on bedding plants for big splashes of color and form. The Victorians popularized the gardening method called "change bedding"—the art of planting lavishly for a temporary show and switching out plantings, depending on plant life cycles or personal whims. You'll find options for seasonal bedding-plant replacements at a local garden center in six-packs or flats. The most familiar and easy-to-find plants are annuals and tender perennials, which won't survive frost but will do most of the work in the garden for you. Many bloom on and on, from spring through fall, spreading vigorously. Of course, plants require watering when the soil begins to dry, especially when they're getting started. If they appear droopy or lackluster, give them a drink. For bigger, more beautiful results, feed them every week or two with all-purpose, water-soluble fertilizer.

Viola × wittrockiana 'Universal Plus'

Pelargonium × hortorum 'Orbit Hot Pink'

Petunia 'Hulahoop Hybrids'

Impatiens Super Elfin hybrids

Solenostemon 'Wizard Hybrids'

Making a No-Dig Bed

1

2

3

4

5

> **"PACKAGED GARDEN SOIL** is specially designed to work in flowerbeds the same way a potting mix works in pots. Ironically, native soil from the garden, no matter how productive and earthworm-laden, does not perform as well in pots or containers."
>
> —Peter Strauss

A NEW GARDEN arises from a raised bed built of weather-resistant cedar lumber. Assemble the frame in place and plant it the same day.

1 Using 2×6×58-inch pieces, make two square frames, butting the ends in opposite directions. Stack the frames and fasten them with 2×4×11-inch uprights at intervals.

2 Attach 2×4×11-inch uprights adjacent to the corners. Place a 2×2×11 at each corner. Attach 2×2s to the bottom edge of the frame, in between the 2×4s. Top each side with a 2×4×60-inch piece to form a ledge.

3 Cover the bottom of the raised bed with a 6-inch-deep layer of topsoil. The underlying turf will deteriorate gradually into rich soil.

4 Add a 6-inch layer of garden soil.

5 Blend the soils using a shovel. The soil mix encourages plant roots to reach beyond the depth of the bed and into the ground. Deep-rooted plants draw on subsoil moisture and are thus better able to tolerate and even thrive in dry weather.

Rose Arbor Romance

Glamorous and graceful, a rose-draped arbor epitomizes the romantic garden. Between the architecture and the heady fragrance of the flowers, beauty is abundant.

Call it an ideal marriage. By pairing an arbor and a climbing rose in a garden, you'll make a romantic fantasy come true. The structure gives the plant the support it needs to reach its potential while raising the blooms to more enjoyable levels. Climbing roses typically grow from 6 to 20 feet tall and need sturdy support to keep them from flopping over and looking chaotic. Although most rose canes have thorns, they won't cling to a trellis or twine over a support as a vine would.

Encourage the relationship between an arbor and a climbing rose by coaxing the canes to hug the structure and sprawl over it.

Even on its own, an arbor stands out as a vertical garden element with multidimensional appeal. It marks an entryway and frames a view. As a portal to the house and garden, it represents an open invitation and beckons visitors. By reinforcing the mystery of what lies beyond it, an arbor brings drama to the setting, increasing its appeal.

Plant the same rose on each side of the arbor, or different ones. It takes several years for climbers to cover a structure. To hasten a lush look, plant an annual vine (cardinal climber or black-eyed Susan vine) for quick coverage the initial year, or, for year-to-year tandem growth, a perennial vine (clematis or hops).

▲ Loosely Tie Canes
As canes grow, lash them to their support using flexible ties, such as twine or strips of old stockings. Avoid using wire; it inevitably cuts or strangles the canes.

▲ Prune Lightly
Climbing roses routinely need pruning only to remove dead and spindly canes (those smaller in thickness than a pencil). Cut out some of the oldest canes yearly, as part of garden cleanup in early spring.

▲ Some Roses Are Really Easy
Choose an easy-care climbing rose, such as 'John Cabot', which has natural disease-resistance, only minimal pruning needs, and, for cold climates, cold-hardiness.

Materials and Equipment

- One 4'×8' cedar arbor kit
- Dark green and black exterior stains
- Four metal post-anchor stakes
- Concrete mix (optional)

The Plants
shown on the opposite page

- One bare-root (or container) 'John Cabot' climbing rose (red)
- One bare-root 'New Dawn' climbing rose (pink)
- One 3" golden hops vine (optional)

Plan of Action

1 Find a site for the arbor, such as an entryway to the house or garden, which receives at least six hours of sun daily. Climbing roses do best in a sunny place with well-drained, enriched soil.

2 Select an arbor (either a kit, ready-made, or built from scratch). Select plants, depending on your preference for color, texture, bloom time, and maintenance needs. Choose plants that suit the climate you live in.

3 Build the arbor and install it. The arbor-from-a-kit shown includes post-anchor stakes for securing it. If you prefer, sink posts in 6-inch-deep holes, and fill the holes with concrete.

4 Plant a rose on each side of the arbor. Plant one or two vines, too, if you like.

5 As the roses develop, train the young canes while they are pliable by tying them at strategic points with loose, flexible ties. Feed regularly with plant food for roses.

Soft red 'John Cabot' is an exceptionally cold-hardy reblooming rose that has fragrant, fully double flowers all season. If paired with the clear pink of 'New Dawn,' another hardy climber, the arch will seldom be without flowers from early summer until frost.

Great Climbing Roses

A 'JOHN CABOT' was developed in Canada for winter hardiness. It is also resistant to mildew and black spot. The double, light red flowers are a soft color that looks beautiful anywhere. Hardy in Zones 3–9.

B 'NEW DAWN', is a vigorous, hardy, and disease-resistant climber. The lightly scented, pale pink blooms appear in flushes late spring to fall. Thorny canes can reach 20 feet. Hardy in Zones 4–10.

C LADY BANKS ROSE is for warm to hot climates and is synonymous with Southern gardens. The canes are nearly thornless. Yellow or white forms have scented blooms in spring only. Hardy in Zones 8–11.

D 'MME ALFRED CARRIERE', an old rose dating to 1879, produces creamy white blooms with a heady rose fragrance over a long season, even through winter in the South. Hardy in Zones 7–11.

E 'BLAZE IMPROVED' is as subtle as a fire truck and popular for its reliability. It's everblooming and slightly scented. It grows rapidly and tolerates some shade in good soil. Hardy in Zones 5–11.

By virtue of their long, fast-growing canes, climbing roses make perfect partners for arbors and other upright structures. You can train climbers to reach up a wall and over a roof or into a tree. Plant them alongside a pergola, a gazebo, or the sunny end of a porch.

During hot, dry spells, water young plants weekly. Feed plants during the growing season. Use a plant food blended especially for roses, following label directions. Stop feeding in late summer so the wood ripens before winter.

In late winter or early spring, prune to remove any dead, damaged, or weak canes. If your rose blooms only once in spring, cut some of the oldest canes to the ground after they flower.

Rosa 'John Cabot'

Rosa 'New Dawn'

Rosa banksiae lutea

Rosa 'Madame Alfred Carriere'

Rosa 'Blaze Improved'

Planting a Bare-Root Rose

1

2

3

4

5

6

IN EARLY SPRING or fall, plant bare-root roses as soon as you get them. Do not leave sealed in shipping cartons. If necessary, store in a place that is cool but above freezing and out of direct sun. When handling roses, wear heavy-duty leather gauntlet gloves to avoid injury from thorns.

1 Soak roots overnight in a bucket of water that you've enhanced with a splash of starting plant food (follow product label instructions).

2 Dig a 1- to 2-foot planting hole. Amend backfill with bagged garden soil formulated for roses.

3 Mound backfill in the bottom of the planting hole to support roots. Fill the hole halfway. Check the depth of the graft union just below the canes: You want it to be 1 inch below ground in Zone 6 and colder; 1 inch above soil level in Zone 7 and warmer.

4 Use the water enhanced with starting plant food to water the planting and settle the soil. Let the water soak in, then add more soil if necessary.

5 Make a shallow moat around the plant to collect water. Mound more soil around the canes to 12 inches high to keep canes from drying out.

6 When the days warm and the plant begins to grow, rinse the soil mound away from the canes.

"**ROSES ARE SOLD BARE-ROOT** in spring. Look for plump green stems at least as big around as your little finger. Avoid heavily waxed canes, blackened canes, or signs of fungal diseases. If you miss out on the bare-root bushes, roses are sold already potted and growing in containers all season. If you buy in bloom, you can check for color and fragrance."

—Peter Strauss

Put big, bold plants to work in your yard to turn an eyesore into a place of beauty. Tropical plants grow in a hurry, so nurseries can often provide a lot of greenery for little money. These huge palms were purchased at a home center for less than $30 each!

As shown in the before photo *(below right)*, "no-man's-land" describes the sad strip of grass struggling to pass for a lawn. It's located between a driveway and a brick dining terrace next to the back door of the house.

BEFORE

Backdoor Makeover

What family wants to greet a patch of scraggly lawn between the driveway and the backdoor every time they come home? Here's an easy makeover.

What do you see when you come home from work and get out of your vehicle? If it's an eyesore, or existing plantings are struggling, here's where you can spend a little effort and money and feel good about it every time you come and go. The "before" picture shows a strip of weeds and grass trying to pass for a lawn in an area about 4 feet wide by 15 feet long. It is situated between the drive and a bricked dining terrace onto which the back door opens. Constant foot traffic stresses the grass.

The solution is to remove the grass and any other vegetation, along with the roots and soil, to a depth of 3 inches. Stand bricks on end all around to frame the area. Lay down a weed barrier, then fill in with mulch. Add three palms in 18-inch pots plus one 8-inch pot of colorful coleus. The result is a place that makes homecoming an uplifting event instead of a downer.

As a bonus, these palms look good indoors in winter. Place them near any sunny window.

▲ **Roll Out Landscape Cloth**
Clear the bed of weeds and any rubble. Level the soil and tamp lightly. Position landscape cloth, which prevents stubborn weeds from regrowing.

▲ **Stabilizing**
Steady pots against wind gusts by adding ballast—two to four bricks, a couple of fairly hefty rocks, or a layer of coarse gravel in the bottom of each pot.

Materials and Equipment

- Three 18" polystyrene claylike pots
- Two large bags of premium potting mix
- Stakes and twine
- One 50-pound bag of river gravel for mulch
- One 10'×3' roll of landscape cloth (or to size as needed)
- Bricks to edge bed
- Bricks or rocks for ballast in pots
- One 8" standard clay pot
- Three 50-pound bags of cypress (or other) decorative bark mulch

The Plants
shown on the opposite page

- Three 6' palms in 3-gallon pots
- One pink-and-red coleus in starter pot
- One copper-and-lime-green coleus in starter pot

▲ **Mulching**
Mulching the soil in a pot gives a tidy finish that is also hardworking: A mulch of river gravel keeps soil from splashing out, conserves moisture, and adds weight for pot stability.

Plan of Action

1 Define the area using stakes and twine.
2 Remove exisiting vegetation, roots, and soil to a depth of 3 inches; level with a rake.
3 Sink bricks halfway into ground, standing on end all around, to frame the area.
4 Install landscape-cloth weed barrier (see photo above right). Fill with mulch.
5 Repot palms; transplant coleus to one pot.
6 Water to keep moist; feed every two weeks with all-purpose plant food.

Tropicals Outdoors

TAKE ADVANTAGE OF the large tropical foliage plants available at big-box stores for small bucks. Dramatic, flaring palms create an instantly snazzy look in your garden for as little as $10 each, and they don't require special care. Get the tropical look without planting a jungle. Choose plants for their exciting colors, textures, or shapes, then compose an inviting outdoor living area with a few well-placed potted specimens. Turn your garden into a tropical oasis by tucking the pots of bold foliage among flowering annuals, perennials, and ornamental grasses. Although tropicals hail from frost-free parts of the world, they fare well in most gardens during summer, especially where heat and humidity prevail. A big advantage of these tropicals is that they need little care, only water and occasional feeding. Move plants indoors before frost and keep them in a sunny place until warm weather returns, or leave them to the elements and start over again next season.

A ARECA PALM is easily propagated and grows quickly, traits that keep prices low. Keep the soil moist. Place in part sun to part shade. Bring indoors ahead of freezing temperatures.

B CROTON is prized for flamboyantly colored leaves on woody stems. It tolerates full sun to shade. Protect from freezing. Moist soil and all-purpose plant food will keep the leaves lush and bright.

C DRACAENA is best known as the corn plant for the appearance of its subtly striped leaves. Other varieties have variegated leaves or a spiky appearance. Tolerant of low to high light.

D PHILODENDRON, especially the kind that has large split leaves, makes a big tropical statement in any garden. Grow in part sun to shade, and water as needed to keep roots moist during dry weather.

E CORDYLINE is a dracaena relative. The Hawaiian Ti plant shown here comes with vivid pink leaves; other varieties form green or bronze leaf fountains favored for urn centerpieces.

Chrysalidocarpus lutescens

Codiaeum variegatum var. pictum

Dracaena marginata 'Tricolor'

Philodendron 'Xanadu'

Cordyline terminalis 'Lilliput'

Preventing Weeds

FAR LEFT: Sprinkle a dry, granular weed preventer on soil between plants; moisten with a gentle spray of water.

LEFT: Yank unwanted tree seedlings after a rain; wet soil is more giving than dry earth. A vise grip is an excellent tool for getting a good hold.

BELOW, FAR LEFT: Carefully apply coarse spray of nonselective herbicide on poison ivy and keep it off nearby desirable plants; avoid drift!

BELOW, CENTER: Use a trigger sprayer to direct selective herbicide into the center of a broadleaf weed in the lawn.

BELOW: Hoeing weeds in a vegetable bed is easiest when the hoe is sharp.

A weed is a matter of opinion. Although you may delight when violets and dandelions bloom in your yard each spring, your neighbor may detest these "weeds."

Mighty oaks from tiny acorns do grow, but you probably don't want an oak tree rising from your perennial bed. Considering that squirrels and birds are among nature's most prodigious planters of trees, shrubs, and vines, you'll probably want to undo some of their handiwork.

When unwanted plants, such as plantain or crabgrass, compete with your garden for food, water, and light, it's time to take action. Weed control methods abound: Everything from pulling by hand to uprooting with a tool—even burning expansive areas to employing foraging chickens—has been tried and tested. Smothering with a blanket of mulch or landscape cloth often works. Close planting also helps prevent weeds.

Some of the most effective weed controls are chemical herbicides, which inhibit the growth of weeds or kill them. A selective herbicide kills only certain plants, whereas a nonselective herbicide kills any plant it contacts. Obey all product label instructions.

> **"TRY NOT TO THINK OF WEEDS AS A CURSE.** Botanists maintain that a weed is merely a plant out of place or whose merits have yet to be discovered. I know that as a gardener it makes me feel good to pull some weeds or to slice through their root systems with a good sharp hoe."
>
> —Peter Strauss

Front Porch Seasonals

It takes only a few minutes to decorate your front entry. You can change the look with the seasons or for special occasions and holidays.

▲ **Gentle Dragons Live Here**
'Dragon Wings' begonias bloom all summer with little care other than regular watering and feeding.

▲ **Mums Celebrate Fall**
In autumn, yellow chrysanthemums take over as cheerful sentries until winter.

Large faux sandstone urns, placed on each side of the front door, make substantial sentinels that welcome visitors with stately beauty. The lightweight polystyrene containers look good enough to stand alone, but when they hold pretty displays of seasonal plants or cut flowers, the effect is win–win all around.

For instant success, place nursery pots of fully blooming plants into the graceful urns that stand ready at the doorway year-round. Let the seasons, a special occasion, or a holiday inspire a change. Lift out one potted plant and replace it with another. With a little more effort, arrange in the containers bouquets of fresh flowers and greenery cut from the garden. Place a plastic bucket inside each urn; firmly fit floral foam into each bucket to assist with arranging cut stems and holding them in place. Fill each bucket with water and start tucking in the stems.

Polystyrene urns are available in a variety of styles and colors. Some resemble concrete; others, terra-cotta or carved sandstone. They withstand all kinds of weather and resist the chipping that clay pots suffer from the freezing and thawing cycle. To stabilize against wind, place two bricks or some rocks in the bottom of each urn, or fill the urn halfway with sand or garden soil.

Materials and Equipment

- Two 19"×29" sandstone-look polystyrene urns
- Four brick pavers, or one bag of sand, or one bag of garden soil

The Plants
shown on this page

- Two 10" 'Dragon Wings' begonias
- Two 10" yellow chrysanthemums
- Two 10" large-flowered hydrangeas
- Flowers and greenery, cut from the garden or purchased

Plan of Action

1 Set the urns at the front entry. Add weight (bricks, rocks, sand, or garden soil) to the containers to prevent them from toppling over in a windstorm.
2 Set a pot of colorful blooms into each urn. Change plants with the seasons. A hardy evergreen, such as ball- or cone-shaped arborvitae, works well in winter. Or you can use cut evergreen branches and hollies for the holidays.
3 For a special occasion or holiday, arrange a bouquet of cut flowers and greenery in each container.
4 It's fine to leave the containers empty sometimes; an empty urn or pot symbolizes hope for the day when the perfect plant is found to fill it.

▲ **Hydrangeas Welcome Summer**
Mother's Day and hydrangeas signal the beginning of a new outdoor living season.

BEFORE

In preparation for a party, armloads of yellow lilies, lavender gayfeather (Liatris), magenta snapdragons, and ornamental grasses were gathered from the garden. To make the arrangements, a plastic bucket, fitted with floral foam and filled with water, was set into each urn.

Seasonal Drop-Ins
For Container Gardens

A FAN FLOWER is an annual with swooping, trailing stems covered with blue, purple, pink, or white fan-shape flowers. It's a good edging plant that thrives in sun and heat. Feed with all-purpose, water-soluble plant food weekly. Keep moist.

B BACOPA is an annual with dainty white, pink, or lavender flowers on cascading or billowing stems. It does best in partial shade and moist (not wet) soil. Weekly feeding keeps growth lush and flower-covered.

C FLOWERING KALE is a lacy-leaved counterpart to its ruffled ornamental cabbage cousin, with 10- to 15-inch rosettes in bright colors. Plant in full sun and moist soil; it thrives in cool weather.

D PLECTRANTHUS is a versatile and vigorous, nearly fail-safe foliage annual that offers rich colors and textures plus refreshing scent in exchange for a little water and a half day or more of sun.

E CALADIUM offers wild-patterned, bright-colored foliage. It grows from tubers and thrives in warm weather, moist soil, and part shade to nearly full sun. Dig tubers before frost and store them in a cool, dry place over winter.

DRESSING UP A FRONT ENTRY with containers is as easy as putting on a new hat. First, stroll through a garden center and scan the prospects. If you don't have a planting scheme in mind, mix and match plants in a shopping cart. Focus on candidates in six-packs or 2- to 4-inch pots in combinations; select larger pots or hanging baskets filled with just one kind of plant for a simpler look. Or buy one plant that's large enough to set the pot into the display container at home and you won't need to transplant.

Group plant colors to create a theme, match your home's decor, or make a vivid expression of the season. Choose various plants for an elegant, single-color scheme. Mingle similar-size plants for a uniform effect or arrange ones with varying habits as you would a class portrait: tallest in the back or center; shortest and trailers at the perimeters. Mix fine-texture flowers with coarse-texture foliage or whatever appeals to your eye.

Scaevola 'Blue Wonder'

Bacopa 'Snowstorm'

Brassica oleracea 'Chidora Red'

Plectranthus argentatus

Caladium 'Postman Joyner'

Choosing the Right Soil for Containers

Native soil
Heavy; problematic; too much clay or sand. Not recommended

Topsoil
Heavy; does not retain moisture well; lacks nutrients

Ordinary potting mix
All-purpose; lacks nutrients

Premium potting mix
Lightweight; includes plant food and other enhancements

▲ Your choice of potting soil is important because it affects plants' ability to survive or, better, to thrive. A planting trial demonstrates how the same plant variety performs in four different soils. The ultimate potting soil yields the biggest, most lush plants possible. Choose a premium, enriched potting mix that's made for container plants and packaged for convenient use. Store in the bag or in a lidded plastic, galvanized, or enamel storage container for handy access.

Make sure the packaged potting mixes you use provide the proper proportions of nutrients, moisture, and air that plants need to thrive. Ordinary packaged potting mixes won't do the job as well as premium potting mixes, which contain a variety of enhancements such as plant food for more vigorous growth, wetting agents for good water penetration, sphagnum peat moss and/or coir fibers for extra water retention, and other ingredients that make them lightweight, porous, and suitable for containers. Specialty mixes made (and labeled) specifically for plants such as cacti include ingredients that suit those plants (sand, gravel, or ground limestone, for example).

The planting trial shown above illustrates the effectiveness of various soils. Heavy when wet, even good native soil from the garden drains poorly in a pot and lacks sufficient nutrients. It may harbor weed seeds, disease organisms, or insects. Packaged topsoil is also heavy and holds moisture to the exclusion of the oxygen roots need.

Packaged garden soil is designed especially for amending in-ground garden beds, and contains sphagnum peat moss and manure. Compared to ordinary potting mix, a premium potting mix contains added nutrients to give seeds and plants a strong start—but all mixes need regular feeding later in the season.

"ALWAYS USE PREMIUM POTTING MIX when growing container plants. Roots can't forage beyond container walls for what they need. Fresh premium potting mixes include space-age enhancements that give your plants a head start for optimum growth."

—Peter Strauss

BEFORE

◀ A gated garden entry appears to welcome, but the concrete-block steppers and meager grass really say "stay out" (left). After installing a bottle-glass "mat" interplanted with creeping thymes, the setting offers an irresistible invitation to enter and see what lies ahead.

Garden Gate Upgrade

Lay out a beautiful threshold that welcomes visitors with a carpet of colored glass and fragrance with every step.

A green glass welcome mat cushioned with aromatic creeping thymes is a beautiful, friendly complement to a lattice arbor, picket fence, and garden gate. Planting wine bottles in your garden won't result in grapevines, but you'll harvest accolades for your efforts.

This garden rug, designed to fit under the arbor and in front of the gate, uses wine bottles in a variety of green-glass hues, thus creating an interesting pattern in their placement. It's an ingenious way to recycle empty wine bottles or other colorful glass bottles that have been piling up in the basement, the garage, or at your neighbor's house. Blue glass makes a showy rug, but blue bottles are not as common as green. Nonetheless, amass as many bottles as you think you'll need to make a welcome mat that's a suitable size for your garden's entryway, whether or not it features a gate or an arbor. There's no need to remove the bottle labels. Cheers!

▲ **Digging the Groundwork**
A layer of sand and a sheet of plywood form a sturdy base for the welcome mat that's designed to drain moisture and resist settling.

Materials and Equipment
(to make one 4'×2' welcome mat)

- 48 empty wine bottles
- Garden shovel
- Square-tip spade
- One 4'×2' piece of ⅜" plywood
- Three 50-pound bags of sand
- Two 4' lengths of plastic garden edging
- One 40-pound bag of garden soil

The Plants
shown on the opposite page

- Four 4" creeping thyme
- Four 4" golden thyme
- One package sweet pea seeds
- Two grape plants

Plan of Action

1 Decide where to place the garden rug. Gather building materials. Measure and mark the area for excavation.

2 Dig a 4×2-foot hole approximately 14 inches deep, using the shovel and spade. Level the bottom of the hole by covering it with a 2-inch layer of sand. Place the piece of plywood on top of the sand to form a barrier that keeps the bottles at the same level and prevents them from settling over time. Pour a 4-inch layer of sand on top of the board to hold the bottles in place.

3 One by one, row by row, sink the bottles neck down into the sand, allowing 2 inches between bottles. Place them with their bottom an inch above ground level. Sprinkle soil in between the bottles to hold them in place, then fill the remainder of the hole to 1 inch from the bottom of the bottles.

4 Remove plants from nursery pots and gently divide them into smaller plants. Tuck their roots between the bottles. Hammer in garden edging along the front and back boundaries of the rug to keep soil in and grass out.

5 Plant grapes and sweet pea seeds at the base of the arbor and picket fence.

▲ **Bottles Go in Bottoms Up**
Stagger rows of same-size bottles in the layer of sand. Position them 2 inches apart and adjust them if necessary to make a level surface for walking.

▲ **Set Plants You Can Step On**
Fill in around the bottles with soil and creeping thyme. Leave the bottoms of the bottles just above ground level, so they won't get lost among the plants.

Fragrance Underfoot

A CREEPING THYME grows in part shade to full sun. Keep soil moist, but not wet, until the roots take hold. After it is established, creeping thyme is drought-tolerant. Many different scents and leaf colors are available. Hardy in Zones 5–10.

B CORSICAN MINT is menthol-scented and the smallest of the true mints; the individual leaves are tiny. Provide moist soil and light shade. Shield corsican mint from encroaching neighboring plants, which can easily overwhelm it. Hardy in Zones 7–10.

C CHAMOMILE needs sun and good drainage and does best when grown between stepping-stones so its delicate leaves aren't trampled on. You can mow chamomile like a lawn. The dried flowers are used for tea. Hardy in Zones 4–10.

D WOOLY YARROW is a vigorous perennial with soft, finely cut gray-green leaves all season and yellow blooms in early summer. It tolerates drought and neglect but needs full sun. Hardy in Zones 3–10.

E GOLDEN OREGANO has bright, glowing yellow-green leaves on half-upright to trailing stems. It benefits from light shade in hot-summer climates. Periodic shearing keeps the plants tidy and colorful. Hardy in Zones 5–10.

Creeping or mat-forming herbs are among the multitudes of groundcovers that gardeners turn to when they need plants to fill in between pavers, stepping-stones, or glass bottle bottoms (as in the garden rug on pages 32–33). You'll find numerous creeping varieties of popular herbs, such as thymes and mints, which form a cushion underfoot without covering up the steppers.

The strength of most herbs is in their leaves. If you step on the plants or brush against them, their fragrance is released. As a bonus, many herbs produce lovely, albeit not particularly showy, flowers. In general, snip flowers off plants when they finish blooming to promote fresh-colored new growth.

Until creeping herbs develop and cover an area, water them every other week in the absence of rain. Pull any weeds that invade the planting area. Herbs in general need sun and well-drained soil but only occasional, light feedings to keep the plants vigorous.

A
Thymus 'Victor Reiter'

B
Mentha requienii

C
Chamaemelum nobile

D
Achillea tomentosa 'Aurea'

E
Origanum vulgare 'Aureum'

Choosing and Applying Plant Food

▲ Use a water-soluble plant food delivered via a hose-end feeder to simultaneously feed and water vegetables and bedding plants.

▲ Use a hose-end sprayer to feed large numbers of container plants with controlled amounts of plant food delivered in a gentle mist.

▲ Dilute concentrated liquid food in a watering can and keep it handy for watering a few containers of roses and other plants whenever needed.

▲ Apply premixed liquid plant food straight from the container onto the soil of houseplants and other potted plants.

WHEN IT COMES TO nourishing plants of any kind, you'll find an array of plant foods and ways to apply them in any garden or lawn situation as well as indoors. Whether all-purpose or plant-specific, each is formulated to promote healthy plants. Application methods depend primarily on the type and form of food you're using.

Consider the two basic forms of plant food: dry and liquid. Dry plant foods come in powdery crystals, larger granules, slow release pellets, and spikes. You'll find liquid foods in concentrated or premixed forms. Water-soluble foods consist of fertilizer crystals or liquid concentrate that is mixed with water. Leaves can absorb this kind of plant food as well as roots. Apply it to the soil, feeding

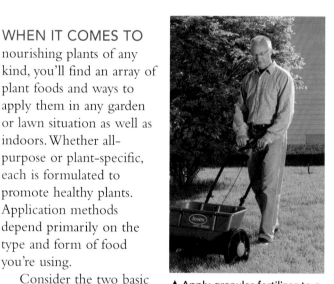

▲ Apply granular fertilizer to a lawn using a spreader to help distribute it evenly and quickly over a large area.

▲ Shake slow release pellets from the container around garden plants every three months. Water well.

▲ Insert fertilizer spikes into soil around the drip line (perimeter of the root zone) under a shrub or small tree.

plants through their roots, and spray it on their leaves as a foliar food. Foliar feeding, however, is not recommended for indoor plants.

Follow package label directions for any kind of plant food to determine when to apply it and how often. Always measure.

"FEED PLANTS REGULARLY AND OFTEN AS DIRECTED. Just as they need sunlight and water, plants need food regularly to thrive. Plant foods lose their potency when exposed to air, so keep bags or containers tightly closed when you're not using them."

—Peter Strauss

In this chapter

38 NO-DIG HEDGE
Combine a low fence and potted plants to make a privacy screen without digging.

40 Plants: Fast-Growing Plants
41 Technique: Containing Invasive Plants

42 FRONT PORCH PRIVACY
Relax in a secluded front porch retreat that's protected by vines growing on a bamboo trellis.

44 Plants: Good Vines for Different Supports
45 Technique: Providing the Right Support for the Vine

46 INSTANT BACKYARD GETAWAY
Create a getaway with a comfy bench and a pair of potted trees underplanted with fragrant flowers.

48 Plants: Standard Shrubs and Small Trees
49 Technique: Growing Trees and Shrubs in Containers

50 BOWER OF FLOWERS
Cozy up any bench with a backdrop of delicate, fine-texture flowers.

52 Plants: Lacy Backdrops
53 Technique: Recommended Mulches

54 A COOL, MISTY OASIS
Make a refreshing retreat for chilling out in times of hot, dry weather.

56 Plants: Shade-Lovers
57 Technique: Understanding Shade and Sun

enclose

Gardens That Enclose

Outdoors in the garden, embraced by nature, you can shape a place where you feel secluded, safe, and comfortable. Garden retreats provide everyone with their own corner of the world.

Define an area to give the garden a sense of enclosure and privacy. Provide shelter, using structures or plants, to make the place more intimate. Here are some quick, low-cost ways to screen a view, shape a backdrop, make an instant retreat, or set up a shady oasis.

No-Dig Hedge

Find privacy in your backyard without building an imposing barrier. Simply pair a low bamboo fence with a few potted bamboo plants.

▲ Pots Make It Easy
Five-gallon nursery pots hide behind a bamboo cane fence. The pots contain bamboo plants that would run rampant if they were planted in the ground.

▲ Cut and Cable Bamboo
Cut bamboo pieces 2 feet long. In each piece, drill holes 5 inches from the bottom and 5 inches from the top. String 1/16-inch aircraft cable through the holes, pull taut, and fasten with #6 ball couplings, as shown.

▲ Steel Rods Anchor the Fence
Every 2 feet, drive steel rods through the bamboo (carefully slipping past the cable) and 1 foot into the ground.

When you sit outside on the patio or the deck, does your view begin and end with a blank wall, a cluster of garbage cans, or a car in the driveway? If watching your neighbors mow their lawn isn't your idea of entertainment, here's an easy solution: a no-dig hedge.

Make a low fence of bamboo canes and place it along the edge of an outdoor living area or a garden. Stand large, potted bamboo plants behind the fence to complete the screen. The 2-foot-tall fence is easy to build and it hides the pots. The solid structure and the lacy hedge buffer the patio from wind, hot sun, and the neighbor's view. It's easy to reinforce the look in your garden by including more containers of bamboo and a simple bamboo structure, such as a trellis or pergola.

Dried bamboo canes provide a building material that looks good and lasts for years. Get them in a standard length and width from a garden supplier. The potted bamboo plants, set behind the fence, add color, texture, and drama. This scheme also takes advantage of bamboo's fast-growing nature. Start with waist- to head-high plants, and watch them form a dense screen within a few months. But beware: When planted in the garden, many bamboo varieties grow out of control, so keep them contained.

Materials and Equipment
(to make one fence 2' high, 4' long)

- Forty-eight 2' bamboo canes (1" diameter)
- Three 3' lengths of 5/16' steel rod
- Four #6 ball couplings
- Twelve feet of 1/16" aircraft cable
- Handsaw, drill, sledgehammer

The Plants
shown on the opposite page

- Four 5-gallon upright bamboo plants for each 4' section of fencing

Plan of Action

1 Measure the site. Figure out how much bamboo and how many plants you'll need.
2 Build the 2-foot-tall fence in 4-foot-long sections; such lengths can be joined and moved easily. Drill 1/8-inch holes through the bamboo, 5 inches from both ends. String 1/16-inch aircraft cable through the holes. Secure cable to bamboo using #6 ball couplings; cut excess cable with wire cutters. (#6 ball couplings are sold at hardware stores and are used for pull chains on light fixtures.)
3 Use a hammer to drive the steel rods through the bamboo every 2 feet, piercing the bamboo knuckles and being careful to bypass the aircraft cable.
4 Install additional sections to make a fence that's long enough to fit your site.
5 Place potted bamboo specimens behind the fence. Water the plants regularly and feed lightly several times each growing season.

If both you and your neighbors can take in the entire view of your backyard at a glance, the area isn't as interesting or private as it could be. Additionally, if the site is exposed to wind, late afternoon sun, or noise from nearby traffic, it's time for a change. This quick fix makes a remarkable change in how the space looks and feels.

Fast-Growing Plants

A BAMBOO comes in two basic types, running and clump-forming. The running types can be highly invasive; the clumpers are easily managed and make outstanding plants for large containers. Hardiness varies widely according to species; some are fully hardy as far north as Zone 4.

B LOOSESTRIFE. Gooseneck loosestrife (shown here) is a perennial 2 to 3 feet tall. It spreads rapidly by underground runners. Creeping Jenny is a mat-forming plant with either green or bright yellow leaves. Its long aboveground runners spread aggressively, rooting at the joints. Hardy in Zones 4–8

C CASTOR BEAN is an annual that in hot weather grows 6 to 15 feet tall in a few weeks. Give it sun and lots of water. Because they are poisonous and sometimes attractive to children, remove the seedpods and put them in the trash.

D PAMPAS GRASS grows 8 to 20 feet tall and seeds freely in hot, windy climates. In parts of the West it is considered a weed; in colder, wetter climates, pampas grass is manageable—but big! Hardy in Zones 6–9.

E MINT comes in many flavors (orange, peppermint, spearmint, pineapple) and spreads aggressively. For best control, grow mint in large pots. Hardy in Zones 5–10

REMEMBER THE STORY of Jack and the beanstalk? When Jack's mother tossed his magic beans out the window, they grew sky-high overnight. Although many plants possess a capacity for fast growth, none reach quite that high. Some can, however, prove desirable because they grow quickly enough to be useful in the garden. Consider the climbers that quickly cover a bare wall or an unsightly shed. Some fast-growing giants tower overhead to form a living wall. Some plants creep and crawl swiftly, filling in under a tree where grass refuses to do the job or covering a slope and preventing erosion. In conducive conditions, fast growers get out of control, sprawling too much and dominating the garden. If so, yank handfuls of roots, shovel-prune part or all of a root mass, rip out vines by the armload, or smother groundcovers with mulch.

Phyllostachys bambusiodes

Lysimachia clethroides

Ricinus communis 'Sanguineus'

Cortaderia selloana

Mentha spicata

Containing Invasive Plants

1

▲To restrain a perennial that spreads aggressively by runners, plant it in a pot. Cut out the bottom of the pot, then sink the pot to its rim. Fill the pot with soil.

2

▲Plant the perennial, such as this brown-leaved loosestrife, in the pot. Eventually, the roots will grow out of the container's drainage hole.

3

▲Because even strong-growing perennials like Lenten rose (*Helleborus niger*) can be crowded, this technique turns aggressive plants into better neighbors for any bed.

Some plants have split personalities that make them desirable one day and despised the next, or one gardener's favorite and another's curse. On the good side, these plants offer valuable assets, such as texture, color, fragrance, or flavor. On the bad side, they survive anything and crowd out other plants, cropping up all over the yard the minute you turn your back. No wonder these plants are called invasives.

The chief offenders are plants introduced from other areas that grow too enthusiastically. For example, *Lythrum* takes over wetlands. In the Pacific Northwest, mature English ivies set seeds, which birds scatter, and the seedlings become weeds. Never let lemon balm, the herb, set seeds lest it become invasive.

Here are some guidelines to maintaining the peace with overly aggressive, or "thug," plants:

- Don't introduce them to your garden in the first place.
- Install metal or plastic edging or even pour concrete barriers before setting the invasive plants into the bed.
- Set invasive plants in a container, then sink it to the rim in the planting bed. Aggressive spreaders such as running bamboo and mint will eventually escape through the drain holes or over the rim of the container.
- Timely thinning, pruning, and deadheading to prevent seed formation can keep invasive plants at bay. Shovel-pruning is a useful technique although it requires constant attention. Slice all around the clump you want to keep with a shovel, then sort out and destroy all the loose pieces of root from the perimeter.

"WHAT'S INVASIVE TO YOU MAY BE MY FAVORITE groundcover or vice versa. In some cases I've had to dig out unwelcome perennial roots and sift the soil. Where annuals are concerned, cut off any seed heads before they ripen."

—Peter Strauss

A simply crafted bamboo trellis with vines trained on it provides a lush screen that offers shade, buffers noise, and enhances privacy.

Front Porch Privacy

Sturdy, lightweight bamboo creates a long-lasting screen. Dressed with a cloak of vining greenery, the structure forms a verdant curtain that provides privacy and shade.

Follow these directions to build a trellis comparable to the 7×6-foot one shown. Adjust your plans according to the specific dimensions of the screen's location.

Drill a hole in the top and bottom of each bamboo pole to accommodate a fastener. Space the upright poles 14 inches apart and nail their tops to a 1×2. Use screws to attach the 1×2 to the porch. To secure the bottoms of the poles to the porch, run a length of nylon twine through each pole and through an opening in the brickwork; tie the twine to secure it.

Form the grid pattern by attaching horizontal poles to the uprights. Space the horizontals 16 inches apart and hold them in place temporarily with strips of duct tape. Lash together the intersections of the bamboo poles with nylon twine and secure with nonslip knots (see illustrations at lower right).

For quick cover, plant a fast-growing annual vine such as morning glory. The growing tips of the variegated Virginia creeper (shown) occasionally need to be coaxed around the bamboo and lightly tied in place. Choose an evergreen, such as jasmine or English ivy, to enjoy an all-year green curtain. Select clematis or honeysuckle for the added benefits of blooms and fragrance.

▲ **Lash Together with Nylon**
Lash the bamboo poles together where they intersect, using nylon twine. Tie nonslip knots, such as those learned in scouting or boating, so the horizontal poles hold firmly in place without any slipping.

Materials and Equipment

- Five 8' bamboo poles, 1" diameter
- Six 7' bamboo poles, 1" diameter
- One 1×2 board 7' long
- Cordless drill, nails, screws
- Nylon twine

The Plants
shown on the opposite page

- One 6" Virginia creeper; or choose any vine (see suggestions above for possibilities) suited to your hardiness zone and exposure (sun or shade).

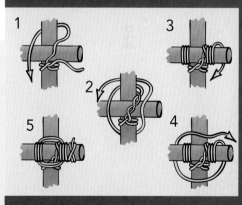

Plan of Action

1 Measure the overall area and plan what size/scale the grid will be. Purchase bamboo poles to suit your measurements and plan.

2 Preview the grid. Lay the bamboo poles on a level area of the yard or driveway. Arrange the verticals, then lay out the horizontals. Make adjustments to the plan, if necessary. Lash the bamboo poles together with nylon twine (see illustration at right and instructions above).

3 Install the trellis on the porch; the procedure is detailed in the text above.

4 Plant vines near the porch where they will reach up and climb the trellis. Water the plants during dry weather; feed monthly with an all-purpose plant food throughout the growing season.

5 Train the plants to climb the trellis. If they don't catch hold on their own, tie them gently in place with jute twine or raffia.

▲ **In Case You Missed Scouts**
Use nylon or poly twine so that it won't deteriorate over time.

1. Just under the horizontal crosspiece, tie a clove hitch around the upright bamboo pole.

2. Wrap the twine three times around both the upright and the horizontal bamboo poles as shown, keeping it taut.

3, 4. Then wrap the twine two times around the horizontal and the upright poles as shown, pulling it tight.

5. Complete the lashing with a clove hitch around one of the bamboo poles.

Good Vines for Different Supports

A MANDEVILLA twines its way upward, as do wisteria, jasmine, honeysuckle, hops, morning glory, and potato vine. Twiners need vertical supports they can wrap around, such as poles or trellises. Never grow them on other plants; they can strangle. Hardy in Zone 10; grow as an annual elsewhere.

B CLIMBING HYDRANGEA clings by means of rootlets along the stems, as does wintercreeper, creeping fig, English ivy, Virginia creeper, and Boston ivy. Clingers can adhere to surfaces such as walls. Climbing hydrangea is hardy in Zones 5–7.

C GRAPE climbs by means of strong, flexible, corkscrewed tendrils that seek out and take hold of narrow supports such as wire, string, or twigs. Sweet peas, garden peas, gourds, clematis, and passion vines also have tendrils. Tendril climbers are best on netting, chain link, or narrow lattice. Most grapes are hardy in Zones 5–9.

D SWEET POTATO is a scrambler, sprawler, and archer without any means of attachment. To assist climbing, tie the vine to a support. Similar vines include bittersweet, thornless roses, and tomatoes. Sweet potato is hardy in Zones 9–10, or grow as an annual.

E BOUGAINVILLEA takes to the air, thrusting upward and outward, assisted by the long, sharp thorns. Tie the sprawling stems to supports. Climbing roses climb in a similar manner. Bougainvillea is hardy in Zones 9–10.

TAKE YOUR GARDEN to new heights. Plant vines in strategic places, then stand back as they perform their acrobatic prowess for climbing. Watch them twine, scramble, clutch, and cling, depending on the plant's technical ability. If you understand how a vine grows, you can help it fulfill its function.

As you consider a vine for your garden, picture its mature height and spread as well as the strength of its potential support. If you have your heart set on a trumpet vine, for example, think about how it climbs by twining along and clinging with rootlets on its stems. You might want to plant it to climb a utility pole at the edge of your property.

A
Mandevilla sanderi 'Red Riding Hood'

B
Hydrangea petiolaris

C
Vitis vinifera

D
Ipomoea batatas Blackie', 'Terrace Lime', and 'Tricolor'

E
Bougainvillea spectabilis

Providing the Right Support for the Vine

▲Sweet peas lash their fine tendrils around lightweight, round supports. Twiggy branch prunings or brush works best.

▲Interplant vines such as clematis and roses for a longer, more interesting season of bloom and fragrance.

▲A strong wire support helps guide a climbing rose up a wall and becomes an invisible but essential infrastructure.

▲Twining wisteria lives long, grows huge, and needs support that is as strong as it is, such as a pergola with heavy posts.

▲English ivy clings to a brick wall without damaging the masonry. Its stem roots act as minute suction-cup holdfasts.

A vine takes on the shape of its support. Good supports need to be able ones, not necessarily fancy ones. Match a support to the weight and strength of the vine you're growing. A twining cypress vine efficiently climbs strings, wires, stakes, or a trellis. Dense or fruiting vines, such as bittersweet, gourds, or tomatoes, need stronger supports that won't topple or break.

Put clingers, sprawlers, and twiners to work hiding eyesores, such as chain link fencing and bare walls. To keep overachievers out of the neighbor's yard, tether them to strong freestanding supports rather than property-sharing fencing.

Most fences and posts or poles benefit from plantings. Besides lattice and trellises, consider using an old ladder or pipes. Use metal or wood to make a strong pergola or gazebo, and make rustic tepees or arbors from slender branches. Anchor thick posts in concrete to uphold heavy loads and withstand rigorous weather. You'll need to keep heavy vines off the house or you'll risk gutter repairs and difficulty painting.

You can also get double-duty with a lightweight vine such as large-flowered clematis by letting it grow up and through a conifer, an old garden rose, or an apple tree.

"USE VINES LIKE A CURTAIN OR DRAPERY. Vines can quickly block out unsightly views and objects over which you may have no control. Use them for a softening effect and to complement otherwise attractive architecture."

—Peter Strauss

Instant Backyard Getaway

Transform an unexciting space into an oasis with a bench and containers of colorful, fragrant plants. Add seasonal flowers to keep the destination freshly appealing.

▲Pockets for Plants
Rings of 6-inch plastic pots form planting pockets or sockets within the display planter and allow instant changes of the garden's colorful underplantings.

▲ Install the Pockets
Place the tree-form standard in the planter, then snuggle the empty pots between its base and the planter. Fill around the standard and between pots with soil.

▲Seasonal Changes
Update the plant display at the outset of each new growing season. Lift out pots of spent flowers and replace them with plants that are coming into bloom.

You can create an outdoor getaway that instantly embraces and encloses. This uncomplicated setting proves as inviting as any full-fledged garden, and it requires little setup or upkeep. Choose a secluded place for your outdoor destination. If you want, it can resolve some landscape problem, such as covering an area where grass grows poorly. Even if you don't have room in your yard, you can locate the retreat on a porch or balcony.

Plant the garden around two small trees in two large planters. Weeping pussy willows trained as tree-form standards are one possibility, or Chinese hibiscus trees for hot weather. Other candidates for potted tree forms include viburnum, flowering maple, and forsythia.

The standards take center stage in the planters; underplantings can be plants with fragrant leaves, such as lavender and lemon verbena. Among these, interplant some 6-inch plastic pots to serve as "sockets," which allow you to remove bloomed-out seasonal plants and replace them instantly with fresh ones that are beginning to flower.

Materials and Equipment

- Heavy landscape fabric (optional)
- Gravel or bark mulch (optional)
- Garden bench
- Two 30" polystyrene planters
- Sixteen 6" plastic nursery pots
- Eight bricks
- All-purpose premium potting mix

The Plants
shown on the opposite page

- Two weeping pussy willow tree-form standards in 3- to 5-gallon pots
- Sixteen 6" pots of plants. Spring: daffodil, hyacinth, Johnny-jump-up; summer: yellow Marguerite daisies, sweet alyssum; fall: hardy mums, dwarf asters. Optional: four each of lavender and lemon verbena.

Plan of Action

1 Consider the potential site's exposure; opt for a location that offers some shade. Where a tree canopy is lacking, station an outdoor umbrella in a sturdy base.

2 Set a bench in place. Or make a garden rug by laying heavy-duty landscape fabric on top of a floor-size square of paltry lawn and spreading a 2-inch layer of gravel or bark mulch over it.

3 If the pots do not have drainage holes, drill one or several in each planter. Place four bricks in the bottom of each planter to add weight and help prevent the potted trees from blowing over. Transplant standards into the planters and fill in with potting mix. Install planting pockets.

4 Choose 6-inch potted plants for their peak-of-glory color and fragrance. Replace plants as flowers fade or when you find fresh, seasonal options at the garden center.

5 Water plants regularly and feed with all-purpose plant food every 7 to 14 days.

BEFORE

Create an instant garden in containers and vary its look as the seasons change. Stage a spring display under weeping pussy willow trees with hyacinths, mini daffodils, and Johnny-jump-ups. Trade these in early summer for yellow Marguerite daisies and sweet alyssum (as shown). Later, put in hardy mums and dwarf asters for a fall display.

Standard Shrubs and Small Trees

A CHINESE HIBISCUS is a warm-season shrub that you can train as a tree. Position in half to full sun. Water to keep soil moist. Feed with plant food for acid-loving plants. Protect from freezing. Hardy in Zones 9–10.

B FLOWERING MAPLE has bell flowers and maple-shaped leaves—hence its name. Treat it like Chinese hibiscus but feed weekly with all-purpose plant food for blooms all summer. Hardy in Zones 8–10.

C SWEET BAY is the *Laurus nobilis* of the herb garden. Give it full sun to half shade. Clip back extra-long new branches to keep a shapely crown. Protect from freezing; this is an easy plant to grow indoors through the winter. Hardy in Zones 8–10.

D FORSYTHIA is usually a big fountain-form shrub, but it is also available trained as a small tree called a lollipop standard. Position in full sun. Prune back oldest branches after spring bloom. Hardy in Zones 5–9.

E ROSE trees, called standards, must be grafted to achieve this special form. They have a 36-inch-tall trunk crowned by the flowering branches. Position in full sun. Water freely and feed weekly with rose food. Most are hardy in Zones 7–10.

Tidy tree-form standards, from 3 to 6 feet tall, make outstanding accents, whether potted or planted in the garden. They're grown from a shrub or tree that usually produces multiple stems but has been trained to develop a strong, single trunk and a lollipop head. You can buy them ready-grown from garden centers, nurseries, and mail-order suppliers. You can also grow a tree-form standard yourself using a simple process that requires some patience but yields a satisfying result. Start with a single strong stem. Insert a bamboo cane next to it and tie together lightly but firmly at intervals of 6 inches. Keep all side branches that start to grow nipped or cut off. When the main stem reaches the top of the cane, cut or pinch off the tip. This will cause two or more branches to form at that point. When the branches are 2 to 3 inches long, remove the tip of each. Continue this process until a rounded, many-branched head has formed. Keep the tree staked to prevent breakage from winds.

Hibiscus rosa-sinensis

Abutilon 'Vesuvius Red'

Laurus nobilis

Forsythia intermedia

Rosa 'Mister Lincoln'

Growing Trees and Shrubs in Containers

1

2

3

4

5

6

SHRUBS AND SMALL TREES, whether shaped into standards or grown in their natural form, look especially decorative when potted. Many, particularly dwarf varieties, do well in containers.

1 Give a shrub or tree a good home in a substantial container, such as a 30-inch polystyrene planter that offers weather resistance. Protect from extreme subfreezing temperatures; move it to an unheated garage through the winter.

2 Add enough premium potting mix in the bottom of the pot so that when the nursery pot is set inside, the tree will still be at the same level.

3 Slide the plant out of the nursery pot. To dislodge, lay the pot on its side and roll it slightly, back and forth, pushing firmly on the pot walls.

4 Set the root ball on the potting mix, and loosen any roots that tightly encircle the outside of the root ball so they can interface with the potting soil. Add premium potting mix to several inches below the rim.

5 Set seasonal flowering plants all around the tree. Or create planting sockets for seasonal drop-ins as shown on page 46. Compact herbs such as creeping thymes can also be planted around a potted tree, or even colorful leaf lettuces in cool weather.

6 Water well after planting and whenever the soil begins to dry at the surface. Daily watering might be necessary in hot summer weather. Feed regularly with all-purpose water-soluble plant food.

"SMALL TREES AND SHRUBS IN POTS that you can move around offer opportunities to change your garden. Mulch the soil or use seasonal flowers to enhance the display and fill in the pots."

—Peter Strauss

Russian sage clouds the air with long-lasting blue flowers in summer, cooling to the eye on a hot day and always pretty with yellow flowers such as coreopsis and yellow-variegated grass.

Bower of Flowers

Create a more beautiful and pleasurable garden by composing a secret hideaway. Romance might bloom along with the flowers in this sensuous setting.

Ideally your garden includes room for daily solitude or a place where you can sit in private and visit with a special someone. It's easy to choreograph a romantic bower of flowers where nothing more than open space once existed.

This design focuses on sensual elements, including plants with fragrance, pastel flowers, and feathery foliage. The Russian sage provides flowers nearly all summer. The ornamental grass contributes a hushed rustle when it sways in a breeze. Groundcovers, combined with a 2-inch-thick carpet of mulch, form a cushion underfoot. The effect is peaceful and soothing.

Choose full-size plants to create instant privacy. Plant a dense group of finely textured varieties to achieve the look of a lacy screen. Use upright arborvitae or English yew as a lush backdrop with soft, aromatic evergreen foliage. Form a hedge either by planting the trees in the ground or in massive decorative pots. A fence, a wall or a mature shrub also offers a suitable background for the protected nook.

The bower pictured includes a bench-size piece of architectural salvage that doubles as sculpture and a place to sit. If you prefer, substitute chairs or a bench. Add a table for an intimate setting for outdoor dining.

▲ An Annual Haircut
In early spring, remove dead parts of porcupine grass. Hold leaves in place by binding them with twine, then shear them off at ground level.

▲ Trim Once a Year
Russian sage is nearly foolproof if you give it sun and well-drained soil. Cut the stems to 6 inches in early spring. That's it!

Materials and Equipment
- One bench-size piece of architectural salvage or other garden bench of your choice
- Two bags bark mulch

The Plants
shown on the opposite page
- Five 12" arborvitaes
- Five 10" Russian sage
- One 10" porcupine grass (*Miscanthus sinensis* 'Strictus')
- One 8" threadleaf coreopsis
- Three 6-packs of groundcovers (such as creeping sedum or creeping thyme)

Plan of Action
1 Determine where you will compose the romantic bower.
2 Install a backdrop of upright evergreens (such as arborvitae or yew).
3 Set the architectural salvage or other seating in place, then prepare the planting bed, adding garden soil and compost as needed.
4 Add perennials, planting them close enough to form a living screen behind the bench.
5 To finish, plant groundcovers at the foot of the bench. Cover remaining open ground around the bench and the plantings with mulch.

Lacy Backdrops

A RUSSIAN SAGE is a perennial with tough but slender stems, deeply cut gray-green leaves, and a cloud of lavender-blue flowers all summer. Give it sun and well-drained soil; it tolerates drought. Hardy in Zones 2–9.

B ARBORVITAE is an upright evergreen that makes a pleasantly scented, dense hedge or background with feathery, bright green foliage. 'Filiformis' is a particularly lacy variety. It grows best in light shade and moist, well-drained soil. Hardy in Zones 3–7.

C SILVER LACE VINE blooms all lacy white on new growth. Cut it back sharply in spring; it will quickly regrow to 20 feet in a single season. It takes the shape of whatever it climbs on. Hardy in Zones 4–8.

D PLUME POPPY is a hardy perennial that grows to 7 feet tall with deeply lobed silver and bronze leaves and feathery, smokey blooms. Pull unwanted seedlings. Hardy in Zones 3–8.

E JAPANESE MAPLE comes in numerous dwarf varieties that make outstanding lacy backdrops in small gardens. They need moist, acidic soil and protection from hot winds and strong direct sun. Most cultivars are hardy in Zones 5–8.

MOST GARDENS BENEFIT from a backdrop or screen of some sort. In addition to creating privacy and shelter from the wind in a garden setting, a screen can hide an eyesore or delineate an area. A living screen of plants, be it a hedge of shrubs planted en masse or a small collection of towering plants, meshes naturally with the landscape. The backdrop becomes a lacy curtain when it includes plants with finely detailed leaves, feathery foliage, or airy branches. Delicate-texture plants combine to form a see-through background that screens the view without blocking it. By allowing a glimpse of the landscape beyond it, as well as sunlight and breezes, a lacy screen provides a gentle sense of enclosure. The overall shape of the plants and the patterns of their parts make the garden more intriguing and possibly dramatic. You can cut Russian sage, silver lace vine, and plume poppy to 6 inches from the ground in spring; they'll quickly regrow in the new season.

A *Perovskia atriplicifolia*

B *Thuja occidentalis* 'Filiformis'

C *Polygonum aubertii*

D *Macleaya microcarpa* 'Kalway's Coral Plume'

E *Acer palmatum Dissectum*

Recommended Mulches

▲ Use pine straw (needles) around berry bushes or shrubs. It decomposes slowly.

▲ Medium-texture bark mulch resists decay and wind. Spread a 2-inch-deep layer around flowers, shrubs, and trees.

▲ Shredded cedar has a fine texture and superior durability. Lay it 3 inches deep on paths and around trees and shrubs.

▲ Sierra red mulch and other color-enhanced mulches are designed to brighten a garden's appeal with all-season color.

▲ Wood mulches colored a rich black help create a feeling of moist woodland that suits azaleas, wildflowers, and hardy ferns.

▲ Dark brown mulches look natural and appealing around all plants and also as the surface for garden paths and walkways.

V arious mulches provide many benefits in the garden. First consider what you want the mulch to do, then choose the appropriate one. Besides neatening the yard, mulch helps retain soil moisture; stabilizes soil temperature; gets plants off to a good start after transplanting; shades soil in summer and insulates it in winter; limits weed growth; prevents soil erosion; minimizes maintenance with less watering and weeding; and attracts earthworms, which aerate and fertilize the soil.

The most common organic mulches include bark (chopped or shredded), pine needles, cocoa bean hulls, and chopped leaves. All of these decompose into the soil gradually, adding organic matter, which is especially beneficial where soil is heavy with clay or too sandy. Some types of mulch, such as wood chips and sawdust, decompose rapidly and draw nitrogen from the soil. If you use these mulches always apply nitrogen–rich plant food.

The ideal mulch is long–lasting and not easily washed away by rain. It has a loose structure that allows water to pass through it quickly and features a color and texture that work well in the setting. For the pathways and floors of outdoor living areas, choose mulch that won't slip underfoot. Pebbles, coarse gravel, and rocks spread on top of landscape fabric make attractive and useful mulches, especially in areas where a lawn is impractical.

"LEAVE A GAP of 2 inches or more between mulch and the trunks of trees and shrubs. This will help prevent the trunks from rotting and being damaged by pests, yet still aid water to reach the root zone."

—Peter Strauss

A Cool, Misty Oasis

Imagine a cool, breezy garden room, full of flowering plants and refreshing, mist-filled air—all in a hot, desert setting. You'll need a structure and mist.

▲ **The Place for Hanging Plants**
Hanging baskets of all kinds will thrive in the moistened, cooled air. Some possibilities include periwinkle, mini petunias, heliotrope, and bacopa.

▲ **Safety in numbers**
Group pots of various sizes so that the different plants complement each other. Here there is blue plumbago, 'Lady in Red' salvia, sweet basil, and hot peppers.

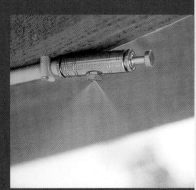

▲ **Misters are a snap to install**
Cool-mist nozzles humidify the air and lower temperatures by up to 20°F. They're adjustable and programmable for misting individual plants or entire areas.

Generations of gardeners have used lath houses as plant shelters that feature a balance of shade and sun, along with freely flowing air. Now there's a whole new variation on this theme, namely the use of inexpensive misters that come in kits and which can be installed up high in a pergola or ramada like the one shown here or in a gazebo.

Plants love the moist air and in any hot, dry situation the mist can have a dramatically cooling effect that makes an outdoor room much more appealing as a place to dine or chill out with friends.

The ramada shown measures 7×9 feet and was built by the owners in about 25 hours. Two mister kits were purchased off the shelf at a home improvement center for about $30 each and required under a half hour to install. The water source is nothing more than a garden hose, which can be operated manually or by an automatic timer.

Summer tropicals are ideal plants for a misty ramada. If the structure receives shade from trees or by a building, select shade-loving plants such as ferns and philodendrons. If the area receives mostly sun, select from kinds that thrive in lots of light, such as Chinese hibiscus, plumbago, and duranta.

Materials and Equipment

- Weather-resistant lumber (cedar) for building the ramada
- Two mister kits, 4 feet of 3/8-inch hose, and connector

The Plants
shown on the opposite page

- Gallon or larger pots of jasmine, honeysuckle, plumbago, and philodendron
- 6-inch pots of kalanchoe, 'Lady in Red' salvia, petunia, basil, pepper, and periwinkle

Plan of Action

1 Build a stand-alone or lean-to pergola, known as a ramada in the Southwest.
2 Lay a quarry tile or brick floor or opt for quicker, less costly gravel or sandstone pebbles.
3 Install the misters. If using two kits, you will need an extra length of ⅜-inch hose 4 feet long and one junction connection to join the two kits. Tubings pre-cut at 3-foot lengths are joined by brass fittings with the mist nozzles plugged in. Brackets that come with the kits can be nailed or screwed in place to hold the tubing.
4 Run a hose to the pergola or ramada and attach to the mister system using an adapter and simple filter. Turn on the hose and adjust to get the desired misting effect.

Two mister kits at about $30 each and a half hour of installation time turned this pergola or ramada in Phoenix into a cool place to hang out, literally and figuratively. The potted plants include jasmine and honeysuckle for fragrance. There are also kalanchoes, salvias, periwinkles, and edible basil and peppers.

BEFORE

Shade-Lovers

A HARDY FERNS grow 1 to 4 feet tall and thrive in varying shade, especially if they have rich, well-drained, moist soil that has been amended with peat moss or packaged garden soil. Hardiness varies by species.

B REX BEGONIA is a frost-sensitive plant that sends up gorgeous leaves from a thick rhizome near the soil surface. Plant outdoors when the weather is warm and settled. Winter indoors or start from new plants each year.

C PRIMROSES of many colors and different growth habits are prized spring flowers in any garden spot that receives sun early in the season but becomes shady in summer. They need moist soil. Hardiness varies widely by species.

D FOXGLOVE is the popular name for *Digitalis*, biennials that grow basal rosettes of leaves the first year and send up spires of charming flowers the second spring. They like dappled to medium shade. Hardy in Zones 4–8.

E SPURGE is a huge group of plants with beautiful textured foliage. Many are easy to grow and outstanding when you want to vegetate a problem, dry-shade site. Hardiness varies by species.

THE AMOUNT OF SHADE in a garden affects a plant's ability to survive and thrive there. Shade is a broad term with many nuances. Generally a shady site receives less than six hours of direct sunlight daily during the summer. Types of shade include light, dappled, half (or medium), and heavy. Each is more suitable for some plants than others. The shade under deciduous trees and shrubs shifts seasonally, depending on the leaves.

Low light conditions suit a range of beautiful plants, from annuals and perennials to shrubs and trees. Some of the most outstanding include ferns, hostas, hydrangeas, and Japanese maples. The hardy lilies and various kinds of clematis do well with a cool, shady root run, but they must have sun on their leaves for a half day or more. A highly desirable kind of shade (for both plants and people) is the parklike setting found under a high canopy of leaves from tall trees that have had their lower limbs removed.

A
Adiantum pedatum

B
Begonia rex-cultorem 'Escargot'

C
Primula vulgaris 'Pageant Hybrids'

D
Digitalis purpurea 'Foxy'

E
Euphorbia characias wulfenii

Understanding Shade and Sun

▲ Full or deep shade exists under a dense tree or on the sunless side of a hedge, wall, or building.

▲ Dappled shade shifts throughout the day under tall, small-leaved trees, an arbor, or a lath house.

▲ A site with warm, gentle morning sun and afternoon shade or intermittent shadows for the rest of the day is ideal for many shade-loving plants.

▲ Full afternoon sun is hot and harsh in summer, when the sun's rays are strongest. It blisters unsheltered shade-lovers.

▲ If your garden is too shady, remove the tree's lower branches—called limbing up—or hire a professional arborist to do it.

Plants' health depends on light, but with too much sun or shade, plants suffer and die. Those that receive too much sun scorch, fail to thrive, and require constant watering; move them to a shadier place or create shelter for them before it's too late. Without enough sun, plants stretch toward light and become spindly.

Be aware of the conditions that exist in your garden from sunrise to sunset. When you acquire plants, try to match their needs to conditions in your yard. Plant labels and catalogs inform you of a plant's needs for light and shade, as well as soil moisture. Plants may prefer one situation but tolerate another.

Areas of shade or sun are not created equal, especially where there are trees, buildings, and other landscape structures. Different trees cast varying degrees of shade: You'll find light shade under fine-leaved trees with a high canopy and deep shade under evergreens or dense, low-branching trees.

At the edge of a tree canopy or on the north side of a house, plants receive two to three hours of light shade. In cool, wet regions, such a site suits plants described as needing medium shade. In hot desert climates, however, the site is fine for many plants that otherwise prefer full sun.

In this chapter

60 MAKE A TIGHT SPACE SEEM BIGGER
Expand the sense of space in a small area using peek-a-boo mirrors and hanging plants.

62 Plants: Peek-A-Boo Plants
63 Technique: Watering

64 DISGUISE AND DISTRACT: EYESORE TO EYE CANDY
Plant vines to hide an ugly view and guide attention to a beauty spot.

66 Plants: Fast-Growing Vines
67 Technique: Controlling Vines

68 LIGHT FOR A DARK AREA
Cast light in shaded gloom with lime-yellow hostas and silvery lamiums.

70 Plants: Light-Colored Shade-Lovers
71 Technique: Dividing Perennials

72 HIDE THE AIR-CONDITIONER
Here are three quick ways you can safely transform the essential if unattractive air-conditioner into a garden feature.

74 Plants: Evergreens for Hot, Dry Spots
75 Technique: Deciding When to Water

76 WATER GARDEN MAGIC
Surrounded by plants, a simple bubbler fountain in a glazed ceramic pot does the trick.

78 Plants: For a Waterside Effect
79 Technique: Mulching

transform

Gardens That Transform

Celebrate the magic of gardening. Reach into the gardener's bag of tricks and discover how to turn everyday challenges into improvements. Use these strategies to make your garden more beautiful, more satisfying, and less demanding. You'll soon see why some of the most basic gardening techniques help produce the easiest fix-ups in the landscape. Learn how to make a small space appear larger, disguise a shed or an air-conditioner, create light in shady areas, and more. If you plant fast-growing vines, use mulch, divide your plants, and water efficiently, you'll soon have a greener thumb.

Mirrors are one of the most magical of all garden accessories. They create an illusion of space and of gardens awaiting discovery and exploration beyond the looking glass. Just be sure to position them so as not to confuse birds, which may then try to fly through them.

BEFORE

Make a Tight Space Seem Bigger

Hocus-pocus! There's more to this garden than meets the eye. Or is there? This case of visual trickery involves the magic of mirrors.

Like magicians, savvy gardeners practice the art of visual illusion. By deceiving visitors' senses, visual illusion allows gardeners to overcome a small garden's spatial limitations. As a result, the garden seems larger than the small space allows.

In this case, mirrors are used to create a sense of depth. Viewers are fooled into thinking they are looking through windows in the fence. At the same time, nearby plants reflected in the mirrors make it appear that more garden sprawls beyond the fence.

If you like, use the mirrors to reflect a bit of light into a dark area of the garden, such as a shady place beneath a tree.

A selection of see-through plants with fine-texture foliage, such as lacy ferns and astilbes, slightly obscures the lattice-framed mirrors and reflects in them. This design enables you to avoid a problem that commonly occurs when hanging a mirror in the garden: Suspended on a fence or wall, a mirror might lure birds to crash into the reflective surface. Place plants so they help birds avoid collisions and injuries.

You can complete the project in an afternoon. Cut full-size lattice panels into small (14×14-inch) panels, or use scraps of lattice.

▲ **Start with a Lattice Square**
Cut the wood lattice panel so that it measures 14×14 inches. Use an exterior-grade stain to color it to match the fence on which it will hang.

▲ **Well-Placed Dabs Will Do**
Dab heavy-duty construction adhesive around each opening, then lay the mirror on the lattice, reflective side down. Allow the glue to dry before proceeding.

Materials and Equipment
(to make six windows)

- Two 2'×8' panels of ⅛" lattice
- Heavy-duty construction adhesive
- Six 12"×12" mirrors
- Saber saw; exterior-grade stain; cordless drill
- Stain or waterproofing sealer
- Hanging basket, bracket, screws

The Plants
shown on the opposite page

For the hanging basket:
- Three *Helichrysum apiculatum* (outback yellow buttons)
- Three Torenia 'Summerwave'
- Three Salvia 'Navajo Bright Red'
- Three Mimulus 'Princess Jessica'
- For instructions on planting a hanging basket, see pages 150 and 153.

Plan of Action

1 Cut the lattice into six 14×14-inch panels.
2 Stain lattice to match the fence color. Or apply a waterproofing sealer to the wood to help protect it from harsh weather.
3 Attach a mirror to the back of each panel of lattice, using heavy-duty construction adhesive.
4 Mount each window on the fence.
5 Plant hanging basket, install bracket, and hang on fence partially in front of the mirrors. To get the effect illustrated, experiment with placement by moving the basket around until it reflects attractively in the mirrors.

▲ **Mirror, Mirror on the Wall**
Drill a hole in the top corner of each "window" and nail or screw it in place on the fence.

Peek-A-Boo Plants

A BABY'S BREATH comes in both annual and perennial forms that produce wispy clouds of white (rarely pink) single or double flowers. The plants need lots of sun, and soil that quickly drains excess water. The perennial variety is hardy in Zones 3–7

B BLUE OAT GRASS is an ornamental grass that grows 2 to 3 feet tall with narrow blue-green leaves. Plant in moist, rich soil and site in full sun to part shade. Hardy in Zones 5–8

C 'KARL FOERSTER' FEATHER REED GRASS grows into a thigh-high, mostly vertical veil of feathery, wheatlike flower heads. Give it at least a half day of sun and moist soil. Hardy in Zones 5–9

D DILL is an annual herb that grows quickly from seed, first yielding dill weed, then flowering and producing dill seeds. Both seeds and leaves are used in cooking for flavoring. Everything about the plant is lacy and fine-textured.

E 'LAVENDER MIST' MEADOW RUE is a perennial 3 to 4 feet tall that in summer becomes covered with clouds of small, bell-shaped violet flowers at the top of the plants. This is a most elegant plant. Hardy in Zones 4–9.

HERE'S A MAGIC TRICK you'll want to practice at home: using plants to create a visual deception. Choose now-you-see-it, now-you-don't plants with fine stems, wispy foliage, or sheer flowers to frame or screen part of the garden. You see these diaphanous plants standing or sitting at the garden's edge, but you see through them, too, viewing more of the garden or landscape beyond. The shape and texture of the plants catch your attention and let it go in an instant. When light streams through the plants, they appear radiant. Plant a delicate screen in front of a plain fence or other structure to give it a deceptively lively dimension. For ethereal effects, use the plants as specimens here and there in a bed; or dangle them head-high in generous-size hanging baskets. Asparagus ferns and true ferns are often used as a softening scrim in both indoor and outdoor gardens, but many other plants can be used as well.

Gypsophila paniculata 'Bristol Fairy'

Helictotrichon sempervirens 'Sapphire'

Calamagrostis acutiflora 'Karl Foerster'

Anethum graveolens

Thalictrum rochebrunianum 'Lavender Mist'

FAR LEFT: A rain barrel collects water from a downspout and keeps it handy for the watering can. A barrel with a spigot or a hose connector proves most efficient.

LEFT: Hand watering with a hose soaks plants thoroughly. An adjustable-sprayer wand controls the flow with less waste and puts water where you want it.

What is the best way to water plants? It's a matter of what works best for you and your garden. Water conservation is important in any garden and essential in arid regions where drought occurs regularly and water restrictions apply. Many people appreciate the convenience of an automated irrigation system.

Each of the watering methods, whether you sprinkle soil with a watering can or hose or flood soil with an irrigation system, has its advantages. Hand watering guides moisture where it's needed: at plants' roots. A spray nozzle that controls the flow to plants makes watering easier. Sprinkler systems splash water onto broad areas, but they waste water; much of it evaporates before reaching plants. Drip-irrigation systems use porous hoses or small, built-in emitters to drip water onto soil, providing the ultimate in controlled delivery. Irrigation systems with emitters stationed in the ground or in pots can be set on timers and operated automatically. In order to water thoroughly, slow and deep is always preferable to fast and shallow.

▲ A ring emitter set into a big pot at least 18 inches in diameter can help make a rose, shrub, or tree remarkably self-reliant. Plug the emitter into an automated system.

▲ A porous soaker hose lies on or under the ground and weeps moisture slowly, reliably, thoroughly.

"RECYCLE AND SAVE WATER. Remove the bottom of a plastic beverage bottle and half bury it upside down next to a plant you want to be sure is well watered—a tomato, for example. Fill the reservoir with water as needed. The seepage encourages deep rooting."

—Peter Strauss

Disguise and Distract: Eyesore to Eye Candy

Undercover operations use vines and a web of deception to put up a good front while hiding parts of the garden you'd rather not look at.

Sometimes the best solution for a problem is the one that lets nature take its course. In this case, fast-growing vines that bloom at different times climb and spread over a metal shed, transforming it into a focal point of flowers. Disguising the structure, rather than giving up the storage space, turns an unattractive scene into an opportunity. Sweet autumn clematis, a small-flowered hybrid clematis, and honeysuckle complement the shed's broad, vertical support, although the plants rely on netting to climb and cover the structure. Other vines climb and cover via tendrils, twining, creeping, or other specialized adaptations.

Heavy vines require strong support. To fashion a heavy-duty screen, frame a lattice panel, trelliswork, or metal fencing and position it at least 6 inches away from the shed. This tactic allows air and light to reach the plants. Use this freestanding screen to hide garbage cans or a compost pile.

Look for ways to draw attention away from problem areas. Place an attractive object at the edge of a setting where it will upstage the eyesore. Plant a long-blooming, brightly colored rose or a large-flowered hydrangea near a utility box. If possible, paint the offending object a dark color and watch it recede into the shadows.

▲ Stage Your Blooms
For a longer period of effect, let large-flowered clematis (which blooms from late May to midsummer) climb up among the branches of late-summer-blooming sweet autumn clematis.

▲ Know How Vines Climb
Clematis wraps tendril-like petioles around any pencil-thin support (in this case its own stems). Netting provides good support for this kind of vine.

▲ Trimming Vines Is Essential
Remove dead wood anytime you notice it. In spring or summer, trim fast-growing vines such as honeysuckle that are out of bounds.

Materials and Equipment

- Metal (or other construction) storage shed
- Plastic, string, or wire netting
- Screw-in hooks

The Plants
shown on the opposite page

- Two 1-gallon sweet autumn clematis or silver lace vine
- Three 2-gallon 'Annabelle' hydrangea
- One 1-gallon large-flowered clematis
- One 1-gallon trumpet honeysuckle

Plan of Action

1 Determine a strategy for dealing with the eyesore: disguise or distract.
2 For a disguise, choose a vine whose climbing method complements the support. For a distraction, choose a beautiful plant or other object to place in the foreground or nearby.
3 Assist the vine to climb and cover the shed. Use netting (string, wire, or plastic) to support twining or tendril-type climbers on one side of the structure.
4 Hang netting on hooks attached to the structure for easy removal when maintenance or painting is needed.
5 Control overly aggressive vines with annual pruning. Sometime between late fall and early spring, cut back to 6 inches from the ground.

The old toolshed has become a destination beauty spot with its cloak of sweet autumn clematis and the lavish flowering of 'Annabelle' hardy hydrangeas.

Fast-Growing Vines

A SWEET AUTUMN CLEMATIS produces huge billows of small, fragrant white flowers in early fall. It appreciates a shady, moist root run and sun at the top. It's hardy almost everywhere. Zones 3 to 9.

B HYACINTH BEAN is an annual that grows 20 feet in a single growing season. It needs warmth, sun, and plenty of water. The purple flowers are soon upstaged by glowing purple seedpods.

C GOLDEN HOPS VINE is highly esteemed as an ornamental. It's ideal for an arbor or a 6- to 8-foot tepee. Cut the vines to the ground in spring. Hardy in Zones 5–8.

D ORNAMENTAL GOURD vines are hot-weather annuals that grow rapidly to 20 feet and produce decorative fruit. They need sun, well-drained soil, and a strong support that allows the gourds to dangle.

E MORNING GLORY is an annual that grows best with morning sun and moist, well-drained soil. The vines start small but soon take off and grow 10 to 20 feet tall, blooming in late summer and fall. They are an ideal quick cover for a chain link fence.

VIGOROUS CLIMBING PLANTS are among the garden's superheroes. Strong and flexible, they can reach 20 feet or more in a single growing season. These plants prove practical as well as beautiful, if you use them to form screens and disguise eyesores in the landscape. Use quick-growing annual vines in the places you need a cover for a new structure or stand-ins for young perennial vines that will take a few years to develop. Although annuals are destined to last for only one season, beauties such as morning glory, purple hyacinth bean, and scarlet runner bean put on an outstanding show in record time. Some perennial vines quickly reach a mature-looking state and grow out of control unless pruned annually into submission. Trumpet vine and wisteria are good examples of plants that will run amok if you're not careful. Silver lace vine is a leaper, but cutting it to the ground each spring will keep it under control.

A *Clematis terniflora*

B *Lablab purpureus*

C *Humulus lupulus 'Aureus'*

D *Cucurbita pepo*

E *Ipomoea tricolor 'Mt. Fuji Hybrids'*

Controlling Vines

▲ To remove a twining vine such as Virginia creeper from a tree, take it out in pieces starting from the top.

▲ Trimming a vine such as Boston ivy is more about grooming than control; to keep it off windows, pull it out and cut it off.

▲ Be on the watch when a vine begins to extend out from the surface it covers; cut back this unruly extra growth.

Wisteria is a ▶ prime example of a twining vine whose thin new shoots will eventually grow an inch or more in diameter and have the strength to crush wood, but not a metal post like the one shown.

"DON'T BE AFRAID OF VINES. They add a lot of beauty to a garden and sometimes edible fruit. At the first sign a vine is getting too big for its situation, cut it back and thin out some of the oldest parts. Consider some vines for ground covers as well, such as bougainvillea, ivy, honeysuckle, or star jasmine—to name a few."

—Peter Strauss

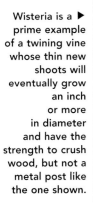

The big appeal of vines is that they take on the shape of what they cover and in record time they can hide or mask out the unsightly. The down side of this pretty picture is that unless vines are disciplined by regular pruning they can become too much of a good thing. It is also important to match vines to appropriate supports. Twiners such as wisteria and trumpetvine may look fetching at the outset on a wood or plastic trellis, but they will soon advance from tender twining shoots to tremendously strong cords and then to wrist-size dimensions with the strength to crush anything but the strongest of supports such as iron posts or more decorative wrought-iron structures. Climbing hydangea and Boston ivy are examples of vines that climb by clinging and remain well behaved until side branches begin to extend out from the surface meant to be covered. Cut these back from time to time so that they neatly drape instead of having side shoots sticking out helter-skelter.

BEFORE

A cavernous area of shade between towering oak trees and a brick building appears lifeless and gloomy even though plants grow there. Adding plants with light-colored foliage brightens the area and, together with a birdbath, invites onlookers to go for a stroll.

Light for a Dark Area

Nestled in the shade of old oak trees and a two-story brownstone, a garden glows, thanks to the light-reflective qualities of plants with colorful foliage.

Magic happens in gardens when you use the power of visual deception to overcome common landscape problems. The goal in this case: Create the illusion of light in a dark part of the garden.

Of all the ways to fool the eye and produce a sense of light in a shady garden, light-colored plants look most natural. Some of the prettiest shade-loving plants include those with variegated, golden, or silvery leaves. Variegation occurs as stripes, streaks, spots, or splotches in contrasts of green and white, ivory, or yellow. Plants with light-colored leaves or smooth, glossy leaves reflect light. As a result, flashes of light and color brighten an area. Light-colored plants also contrast with their garden companions and generate a level of interest that draws you into a shaded area. Put light-colored flowers to work too. The most effective results occur when you combine pastel blooms with their perfect foil: silver foliage.

Structural elements offer other ways to brighten the dark: light-colored mulch compared to dark mulch, for example. Warm-colored walls (ochre or pale yellow) lighten dark corners. A whitewashed wall behind plants produces a more subtle brightening. Place a light-colored arbor at the entry to a shade garden to beckon you in and out.

▲ Assemble the Components
Bring together the plants and the birdbath on the site and try them in different compositions. When pleased with the look, begin the actual planting.

▲ Protect Existing Plants
A plastic bag loosely tied around a bleeding heart will keep it from being trampled while the gardener prepares soil or sets the other plants in place.

Materials and Equipment

- One ceramic birdbath
- One 4' × 8' panel of white vinyl lattice; 1" galvanized screws
- Two bags fine or medium bark mulch

The Plants
shown on the opposite page

- Three 1-gallon Japanese hakone grass
- Three 1-gallon white-edged hostas
- One 1-gallon lime-colored hosta
- One 1-gallon lime-variegated hosta
- Three 1-gallon silver lamiums
- Two 1-gallon bleeding hearts

Plan of Action

1 Define area of shade you'd like to brighten. Attach lattice to fence with screws.
2 Clear the area of any weeds or debris, then spade or fork the soil to a depth of about 8 inches. If clay or very sandy, add compost, sphagnum peat moss, or packaged garden soil at the rate of one 40-pound bag to 6 square feet.
3 Try different arrangements of the plants while they are still in their pots. When the appearance is pleasing, begin planting.
4 Water in the transplants and allow to drain for an hour or two. Then position the birdbath, placing it on several bricks if needed for leveling and stability.
5 Keep the birdbath filled with fresh water. In the absence of soaking rain, water the shade garden weekly, slowly and deeply. Mulch any exposed soil with 2 to 3 inches of bark mulch to save water and help prevent weeds.

▲ Power-Drill Lattice Screws
Use 1-inch galvanized screws to attach the lattice to a wood wall or fence. Place screws every 18 inches for solid fit.

Light-Colored Shade-Lovers

A DEAD NETTLE is a semitrailing plant that blooms in spring but is cultivated for season-long silvery variegated leaves that bring a glint of light to shaded grounds as well as containers. Hardy in Zones 5–10

B HOSTA will grow almost anywhere, but it's best in some shade with moist, humus-rich soil. Look for varieties that have white variegation or leaves that are golden green. Protect from deer and slugs. Hardy in Zones 3–8.

C WINTERCREEPER is a broadleaf evergreen available in varieties having white or creamy to golden variegation. Check labels for habit, which can be creeping or bush-forming. Hardy in Zones 5–9.

D JAPANESE YEW is typically thought of as dark green hedging. There are, however, varieties having silvery white to golden edging in the leaves. It is outstanding for shade as well as sun. Hardy in Zones 4–7.

E PERIWINKLE (*Vinca minor*) is a perennial groundcover, hardy in Zones 4–9, with glossy leaves that reflect light. *Vinca major* is a more tender species with larger leaves and flowers, hardy in Zones 7–9. White- and gold-variegated varieties exist for both species. Provide moist, humus-rich soil in part to full shade.

THE BEAUTY OF WHITE or creamy variegated, golden, or silver foliage lies partly in its ability to lighten plantings in the shade. Light-colored foliage plants work best against a dark background. White variegations make crisp contrasts. Yellow variegations and golden foliage radiate a sunny glow. Silver or gray leaves help blend strongly contrasting plants, and they highlight pastel flowers.

Use light-colored foliage plants sparingly. When overdone, their effects become confusing. Some variegated plants are less vigorous than their green counterparts. Help plants be as strong and healthy as possible by giving them a balance of sun and shade, along with adequate water and food. If variegated- and golden-foliage plants don't receive enough light, their appeal fades along with their contrast or color. Yellow foliage burns in full sun and turns greenish yellow in heavy shade.

Lamium maculatum 'White Nancy'

Hosta fortunei 'Gold Standard'

Euonymus fortunei 'Emerald 'n' Gold'

Taxus cuspidata 'Dwarf Bright'

Vinca major 'Variegata'

Dividing Perennials

DIVIDING PERENNIALS WITH FIBROUS ROOTS

1 Divide a fibrous-rooted plant, such as *Dianthus*, with a fork. Lift it from the garden in fall or at the beginning of spring.

2 Separate the plant into smaller clumps, using your hands to tease them apart. Replant the divisions at the same depth the plant was growing before, but leave room between them.

DIVIDING PERENNIALS WITH FLESHY ROOTS

1 Dig bearded iris or other plants that have thick roots (such as Oriental poppy and summer phlox) in fall and divide. Rinse soil off to see new buds.

2 Break apart or cut new rhizomes from the old clump. Cut off all but 3 inches of each division's leaves. Dip cut parts in fungicide powder. Let dry before planting 1 to 3 inches deep.

DIVIDING PERENNIALS WITH THICK OR WOODY ROOTS

1 In early spring, use a spade to dig a large hosta. Cut through it to make smaller plants; include crowns (pointed shoots) and some roots.

2 Use two forks to pull and pry apart loose sections of rootstock. Replant at the same depth the plant was growing before.

"YOU CAN SAVE MONEY DIVIDING YOUR PERENNIALS. When you are establishing a new garden, there's always a need for more plants. Be a little patient and after the second year most perennials can be divided. Where you had one, all of a sudden you have three and that can add up fast."

—Peter Strauss

Hide the Air-Conditioner

Plant or build a simple screen that conceals an air-conditioner but won't interfere with the efficiency of the appliance as it works to cool your home.

▲ Bamboo Is Quick
Bamboo makes a lightweight and long-lasting screen. It is most appropriate for a Japanese-themed shade garden with a Japanese cutleaf maple, mosses, and hardy ferns.

No one thinks of an air-conditioning unit as an attractive part of a landscape, but few people enjoy summer's heat without one. You can screen the mechanical necessities with plants as shown on the opposite page. Or build a simple lattice construction. Situate the plant or lattice screen at least 1 to 2 feet away from the air-conditioner. It's essential to leave room for the air-conditioner to function properly, pulling outdoor air in through its sides and blasting hot air out through its top.

If you opt for a structural solution, the ideal design is open rather than solid. Aim for a one- or two-sided screen or trellis that leaves room for servicing the air-conditioner without completely enclosing it. Combine a lightweight vining plant with the structure, if you like, but do not allow plants to climb on the air-conditioner.

If trees or shrubs do not shade your air-conditioner, consider adding them to help the appliance work more efficiently. Evergreens offer year-round shade. You might also plant a hedge in front of the unit. For uniformity, choose a plant that reaches 3 to 5 feet and thrives in dry heat, such as an ornamental grass, dwarf juniper, or yucca.

Materials and Equipment

- About a dozen stone or brick paving blocks to define the bed edge
- Four 40-lb. bags of garden soil
- Four 40-lb. bags bark chips or other organic mulch

The Plants
shown on the opposite page

- Three 'Medora' junipers or similar conifer having a columnar shape; select plants 3 to 4 feet tall
- Plants: Five 4" plants each of pentas, lemon licorice, yellow Marguerite, purple petunia, 'Big Ruby' periwinkle, 'Limelight' coleus, 'Rocket Golden' snapdragon, blue salvia

Plan of Action

1 Lay out blocks. With a shovel make marks in soil around the line of blocks and remove turf or other plants. Amend soil with bagged garden soil (one 40-pound bag for every 6 square feet). Turn the soil to a depth of 6-8 inches.
2 Plant junipers so they are about 2-3 feet out from the air conditioner and mulch between them and the air conditioner.
3 Set the blocks in place.
4 Plant out the flowers and apply mulch 2 inches deep between. Water well. Feed plants regularly for best results.
5 Periodically clean out leaves, grass clippings, seedpods, or other plant parts that settle inside the unit to help ensure the air-conditioner's efficient operation. Every spring, before the unit is turned on, use a hose at a downward angle to blast any materials from inside the unit.

▲ Ornamental Grass as Scrim
Calamagrostis 'Karl Foerster' provides a veil of illusion that softens the effect of the air-conditioning units.

Air-conditioning units beg you to hide them from view. A carefully planned and situated screen muffles the noise but in no way hampers the efficient operation of the machinery.

BEFORE

Evergreens for Hot, Dry Spots

A JUNIPERS are suitable for dry gardens, sandy soil, and seaside exposure. There are common and unusual varieties; consider upright, sprawling, or carpeting forms; large, medium, and dwarf sizes. Most hardy in Zones 4–9.

B CYPRESSES are large, fast-growing evergreen trees for mild-winter areas that need little trimming and are useful for windbreaks, screens, or hedges. Consider Arizona, Italian, Leyland, Monterey, or Tecate cypress. Most hardy in Zones 7–10.

C PINE is widely adapted and tolerates both wind and drought when established. Consider Austrian, bishop, jack, mugo, pitch, red, Scots, scrub, Swiss stone, and Torrey pines; most come in a variety of forms, including dwarf and columnar. Hardiness varies according to species.

D ARBORVITAE is notable for softness to the touch instead of prickliness. It is deer-resistant and deep-rooted and is also suitable for shearing. Hardy in Zones 4–8.

E SPRUCE comes in many sizes and shapes and is widely adapted in terms of heat and cold. Bird's nest spruce (below right) makes a dwarf cushion. Colorado blue spruce has a variety of forms and is treasured for the blue color of its needles. Hardiness varies according to species.

EVERGREEN TREES OR SHRUBS retain most of their greenery through the winter, providing beautiful year-round displays. They include a wide selection of exceptional landscape plants in sizes and forms—from sprawling groundcovers to spectacular giants—and decorative foliage in a range of colors and textures. Many evergreens with needlelike leaves are particularly well-adapted to hot, dry locations. Stroll through a local nursery, an arboretum, and your neighborhood to see which evergreens of the conifer type (cone-bearing) do well in your area. Select shrubby or dwarf varieties for small gardens. Help ensure your evergreens' success with proper planting, watering, and mulching. Plant in early spring. For the first several years, until plants establish themselves, water during hot, dry periods and before winter freeze. Deep (12-inch) watering about twice a month encourages a vigorous, deeper root system. Mulch to preserve soil moisture.

Juniperus scopulorum 'Medora'

Cupressus sempervirens 'Stricta'

Pinus mugo 'Kobold'

Thuja occidentalis 'Emerald Giant'

Picea abies 'Nidiformis'

Deciding When to Water

▲ Obvious wilting, drooping, dull leaves, and overall lackluster appearance are signs of thirst. If plants wilt during the heat of the day and perk up in the cool of night, soil is drying but plants can wait for water.

▲ Check the soil for moisture. Use your finger as a dipstick or probe with a trowel. Moist soil feels moist and clings to a trowel. Dry soil crumbles and falls away, dusty and unpleasant to touch.

▲ Deep watering puts water where plants need and use it—at their roots. Drench container plantings until the water runs out the bottom of the pot, but do not leave them standing in water for long.

How much water do your plants need? How often should you water them? Deciding when to water is part of the art of gardening.

The amount of water a plant needs depends on the plant, its stage of growth, and the time of year. Some need moist conditions; others can't stand wet feet. Some ably store water in leaves and stems; others, especially container plants, may need daily watering in hot, dry weather.

A plant's need for water also depends on where it lives. If the climate, weather, and soil conditions spell too much or too little water, it becomes a life-or-death matter. The amount of sun, shade, heat, cold, humidity, wind, rain, and snow all factor into a plant's complex water needs. Heat and wind dry out soil and plant parts. Mulching helps protect them from climatic extremes. Although so-called drought-tolerant plants resist the ravages of hot, dry weather, they still need supplemental watering during their first few years

in the garden. If your garden consists of heavy clay soil that holds water, or sandy soil that drains too quickly, you'll want to improve it. Work organic matter into the soil to help it hold enough water yet drain well.

Always water right after planting. After that, water when the soil feels dry at a depth of 3 to 6 inches for most annuals and perennials, 6 to 12 inches for trees and shrubs. Water infrequently and deeply. Shallow, frequent watering encourages shallow, weak roots. If you water when necessary, rather than on a rigid schedule, your plants will benefit. Ideally, water early in the morning or early in the evening. Watering at midday wastes water through evaporation.

In cold winter areas, give the garden a slow, deep drink before the first freeze to protect from cold injury. Water young trees and shrubs during a winter thaw if snowmelt and rainfall are inadequate. In warm-winter areas, water plants in leaf only if the soil feels dry.

"THE KEY TO HAVING a newly planted, mulched bed settle in and really take off is to water slowly and deeply at the outset. Fast watering displaces mulch, moistens little, and runs off."

—Peter Strauss

There is nothing quite so relaxing in a garden as the gentle splashing or burbling of water. This project is easy and affordable to build. And when you finish, pull up a bench and give your cares a break.

Water Garden Magic

The gentle bubbling of water in an artful fountain brings multiple delights to the garden, as its soothing music and refreshing movement enliven a shady corner.

It's magic, really, that a small, trickling fountain has so much impact in a garden. The water rises and tumbles, splashing quietly, steadily. It attracts birds to the scene, where they stop by for a sip or a bath and chime in with their songs. Nestled between a cozy bench and richly textured plants similar in effect to ones that grow near water, the fountain invites you to sit and savor the shaded setting.

This easy-to-make water feature requires little in terms of time, money, or materials. Select an urn with a substantial base to make a sturdy but statuesque fountain.

Locate the fountain in a secluded, restful, semishady area of your garden where the ground is fairly level and an outdoor outlet is nearby. If you don't have an outdoor electrical outlet with a ground fault circuit interrupter (GFCI), have an electrician install one. It will help prevent short circuits.

Prepare a bed large enough to hold the shade-loving perennials listed below (see page 141 for instructions on preparing planting beds). When planting the perennials, leave enough room for the fountain.

Set up the fountain according to the instructions below. Place the bench next to it.

Cover the ground around the bench and plantings with a 2- to 4-inch layer of bark mulch.

▲ Waterproof the Bottom
Generously apply silicone to the bottom and top of the rubber patch to seal the holes cut for the pump cord.

▲ Install the Pump
Place bricks in the bottom of the urn to set the pump on and to hold it in place. Add a PVC pipe extension to raise the height of the outflow so that it is level with the surface of the water.

Materials and Equipment

- One 19"×20" polystyrene urn
- One small submersible pump
- One 8" to 12" piece of PVC pipe
- One 6"×6" rubber patch
- Tube of clear silicone aquarium sealant
- One garden bench or other seating

The Plants
shown on the opposite page

- Three 6" ferns
- One 8" variegated hosta
- One 8" *Hakonechloa macra* 'Aureola' (Japanese hakone grass)
- Three 4" pachysandras

Plan of Action

1 In the bottom of the container, drill a hole that's wide enough to fit the submersible pump's plug and cord through it.
2 Cut an X in the middle of the rubber patch. Push the plug of the pump cord through the X, then through the bottom of the urn. Pull down the cord until 6 inches remain with the pump inside the urn.
3 Seal the hole: Cover the bottom of the rubber patch with sealant and apply the patch over the hole. Seal the X around the cord. Allow the sealant to dry.
4 Attach PVC pipe extension to the pump and fill the fountain with water. Periodically top off the water as it evaporates or splashes out. Use a chemical ring to prevent mosquito larvae from developing.

▲ Brighten a Shady Place
Golden Japanese hakone grass needs a shady home to prevent its yellow stripes from fading.

For a Waterside Effect

A JAPANESE HAKONE GRASS resembles a small golden-leaved bamboo. It has gracefully arching stems and spreads slowly in moist shade to part sun; it's hardy in Zones 5–8.

B DROOPING SEDGE is a grasslike perennial with gracefully arching foliage and flower stalks. It thrives in moist soil and in half sun to shade. It is hardy in Zones 5 to 9.

C SIBERIAN IRIS blooms for a short time in late spring and early summer, but the clumps of grassy leaves give a pleasant effect the entire growing season. It thrives in moist soil and half to full sun and is hardy in Zones 3 to 9.

D ROSES in the 'Flower Carpet' series are both drought- and disease-resistant. The leaves are a glossy mid-green, and the blooms come in waves from early summer until the killing frost. Feed rose food. Hardy in Zones 4–10.

E WEEPING CHERRY, a smaller tree 8 to 10 feet tall, is available in varieties with weeping branches that arch and cascade beautifully—never more effective than beside a body of water. Hardy in Zones 6–9.

YOU DON'T NEED A BOG GARDEN to achieve the charming effect of a waterside planting. Placed next to a bubbling fountain or another small water feature, ornamental grasses represent the most obvious choice for waterside effects. Gracefully arching specimens mimic water's movement with their flowing, translucent qualities. Stems and flowers rise and tumble over; satiny foliage cascades. The plants dance softly in the wind. Sometimes silvery, sometimes golden or variegated, grasses shimmer in sun and shade. Grasses and other pendulous or weeping-form plants become more visible and effective when placed in front of a plain background. Evergreens or large rocks make ideal contrasts. If the soil in a waterside setting does hold water, choose plants that prefer a boggy place such as acorus or sweet flag and *Lobelia cardinalis*. Promote the water-holding capacity of average soil by digging in sphagnum peat moss or premium packaged garden soil.

A

Hakonechloa macra 'Aureola' with hosta

B

Carex pendula

C

Iris sibirica 'Marcus Perry'

D

Rosa 'Flower Carpet Coral'

E

Prunus subhirtella 'Pendula'

Mulching

◄ Keep mulch several inches away from plant stems and trunks so water can reach roots. Doing so also prevents rot. Keep mulch away from foundations where it could harbor termites. Spread mulch around established perennials (but never over peonies as it buries the eyes too deep) in late fall after the ground has frozen in cold climates. In warm climates, mulch any time.

You and your plants will enjoy the benefits of mulch as it controls weeds, conserves soil moisture, protects plants from extreme temperatures, and adds a finishing touch.

Prepare to mulch in spring. After established plants have emerged and new plantings are complete, fertilize the garden. Water well or wait for a rain. Remove any weeds. Then spread a 2- to 3-inch layer of mulch between plants, keeping the material away from plant stems. The finer the mulch, the thinner the layer should be (you'll use less mulch in wet climates). Mulch again in late fall to help insulate plant root systems from extreme cold in the winter. Mulch potted plants too.

Use compost as free, super-soil-building mulch; you can pile up to 4 inches on the garden every few months. You also can locally acquire other free or low-cost mulch, such as pine straw in the East, chopped corncobs in the Midwest, and hazelnut shells in the Northwest. Call your local waste management or county extension office and ask where mulch is available. See page 53 for types of decorative mulch.

▲ Mulch under trees, beginning a foot away from the trunk. Spread a 4-inch layer in a circle as far as the branches reach.

▲ Pea gravel or coarse grit mulch allows self-sown flower seedlings to take root. Use it for pots of cacti, succulents, or herbs too.

"MY BEST MULCHING ADVICE IS TO GET HELP. When you are spreading mulch between plants, there is nothing like having another pair of arms and hands to hold back leaves and direct what gets mulched and what doesn't."

—Peter Strauss

In this chapter

82 VIOLETS IN THE KITCHEN
Display your African violets where you can enjoy them every day.

84 Plants: Easy Flowering Houseplants
85 Technique: Providing the Right Light Indoors

86 SCULPTURE IN THE GARDEN
Create a sense of discovery with garden art that's nestled into ornamental grasses.

88 Plants: Ornamental Grasses
89 Technique: Edging Between Lawn and Beds

90 FRAMING A VIEW THROUGH A SIDE YARD
Paint a picture in a narrow side yard with a framing arch, a corridor of columnar apple trees, and easy-care roses.

92 Plants: Columnar Fruit Trees for Small Spaces
93 Technique: Planting a Tree or Shrub

94 HANG YOUR GARDEN ON A WALL
Turn a collection of succulents into a work of art: Hang it on a wall.

96 Plants: Favorite Cacti and Succulents
97 Technique: Caring for Cacti and Succulents

98 SMALL-SPACE SOLUTION: GO VERTICAL
Concentrate bunches of showy flowers in a small area with stacked tiers of pots.

100 Plants: Cascading, Spilling Flowers
101 Technique: Catching Plant Problems Early

102 EASY ORCHID WINDOW GARDEN
Enjoy tropical flowers all year with a window garden full of orchids.

104 Plants: Easiest Orchids
105 Technique: Repotting Orchids

106 GROWING CUT FLOWERS INDOORS
Organize an amaryllis extravaganza and watch blooms appear almost overnight.

108 Plants: Favorite Bulbs for Indoor Blooms
109 Technique: Planting and Growing Tender Bulbs in a Container

Gardens That Display

If all the world's a stage, including the garden, you can use the following staging techniques to give plants the stellar treatment. How do you spotlight a star plant? How do you reinforce a garden's drama and frame a view? Should you display plants to focus attention on them by contrasting textures, repeating colors, or playing near against far? Whether you aim for a long- or short-running show, this chapter shows you ways to highlight the assets of ornamental grasses, columnar trees, cascading plants, orchids, and others.

Violets in the Kitchen

Round up a few African violets for the beginnings of a collection. Then spotlight the plants where they're easy to see and tend to while you wait for the coffee to brew.

▲Use African Violet Potting Mix
African violets need a rich but well-drained potting mix. Premium specialty potting mixes ensure an appropriate balance of ingredients for optimum blooms.

▲ Feed African Violets Weekly
When watering African violets, feed them with a water-soluble plant food balanced especially for them. If you feed weekly, do so at half the rate called for on the label. Always water and feed the plants from the bottom. This keeps water spots from marring the hairy leaves.

African violets are among the most popular and collectible flowering houseplants for their variety as well as their blooms.

Once you have collected a few favorites, display them in a group rather than scattering the plants around the house on a shelf here, a windowsill there. Placed in an eye-catching corner of a kitchen counter, for instance, the plants are easy to appreciate every day. They will be easier to water and feed, too.

The setup shown includes an under-cupboard fluorescent fixture that creates bright light for 14 hours a day—just right for African violets. The plants sit on a tray of wet gravel, which increases humidity and helps the plants thrive. Positioned in a warm, cozy corner that protects the plants from chilly drafts, the violets respond by blooming steadily.

If African violets aren't your favorite, a similar setup is ideal for begonias, mini cyclamen, or other houseplants. Simply adjust the timer to alter the amount of light the plants receive. For a less humid environment, use the gravel tray without adding water to it. For a more interesting display, elevate two or three of the plants at different levels on overturned pots.

This "garden" is also a fun place to display cut flowers from your garden or a nosegay of herbs grown in pots.

Materials and Equipment

- One- or two-bulb fluorescent fixture
- One or two grow-light fluorescent tubes
- Waterproof tray for pebbles
- Pea gravel
- Automatic timer
- One bag of premium African violet potting mix
- 5" or 6" ceramic or clay pots

The Plants
shown on the opposite page

- Several African violets in bloom or in various stages of growth
- Small vases for cut flowers

Plan of Action

1 Select a countertop, near an outlet, to set up your lighted plant display.
2 Install a small flourescent fixture above the display area. Attach the light to the underside of a cupboard or disguise it in a wooden frame.
3 Snap one or two grow-light (full-spectrum) tubes into the fixture. Plug the light into the timer. Set the timer; plug it into an outlet.
4 Repot African violets into clay or decorative pots 1 to 2 inches larger using African violet potting mix. This encourages new roots and more blooms.
5 Fill a large waterproof tray with pea gravel. Pour water over the gravel.
6 Set plants on the gravel. Keep plants in saucers to facilitate bottom watering.

BEFORE

You know that dark kitchen corner where the coffeepot resides? You can transform it into a plant display by adding an under-the-cupboard utility light and a tray of flowering African violets. If you like, add cut flowers from your garden or the florist's.

Easy Flowering Houseplants

A AFRICAN VIOLET plants thrive in the same light and warmth people feel comfortable in. Keep the soil nicely moist to slightly dry at the surface. Apply room-temperature water.

B KALANCHOE hybrids are tropical succulents that bloom best in bright light to half sun. Water when surface soil feels dry. Remove dead blooms and rejuvenate plants outdoors in warm weather.

C GLOXINIA grows from a potato-like tuber. Treat the same as its African violet cousin, but provide slightly stronger light. Grows best in warm weather and makes an ideal porch plant in the North.

D HOLIDAY CACTI bloom in fall, early winter, or around Easter, in response to night temperatures below 55°F but not colder than 45°. Grow outdoors in summer. They like fresh air.

E CYCLAMEN grows from a tuber (a bulblike root structure) and blooms for months on end in the same conditions as for African violets, though cooler temperatures are ideal. Avoid pouring water into the heart of this plant.

WHEN MOST PEOPLE THINK OF HOUSEPLANTS, big leafy foliage plants come to mind, but many kinds grow well in pots that can be counted on for a display of flowers lasting weeks or even months. Of plants that bloom seasonally, or in time for the holidays, poinsettias are among those best treated more like a bouquet and discarded when through. Easter lilies grow from bulbs that you can plant in the garden for a future life there. African violets flower nonstop all year. The related florist gloxinia blooms similarly in a warm light garden; if window light is used, spring and summer are the ideal growing seasons. African violets and gloxinia make outstanding porch plants in warm weather. The holiday cacti grow easily, especially if placed outdoors in summer, and they bloom later indoors. Cyclamen are usually purchased in bloom, and they go on flowering in a bright, cool situation. Heat and drought spell their premature demise.

A

Saintpaulia ionantha

B

Kalanchoe blossfeldiana 'Maxi Neon Rose'

C

Sinningia speciosa

D

Schlumbergera bridgesii

E

Cyclamen persicum 'Sierra' (left) and 'Miracle' (right)

Providing the Right Light Indoors

RIGHT: Many houseplants require bright direct light. Here, a cattleya orchid and two cacti bask in strong light. (The brighter the light, the stronger the shadows.)

BELOW: Show off flowering plants within the brightest circle of light cast by a table lamp. It's not strong enough for growing but it is good for showing.

▲ If there is enough sunlight in a room to read a newspaper or do needlepoint without turning on a light, the room is an appropriate place for plants that need low to medium light. Philodendrons, Chinese evergreens, and peace lilies grow well in this kind of light.

▲ Sheer curtains diffuse bright light, making it ideal for African violets, begonias, gloxinias, cyclamen, and ferns.

Generally the amount of light houseplants need is categorized as low, medium, or high. Experiment until you discover where the light in your home suits them best. Some plants survive in low light but need more light to bloom properly. An unobstructed, south-facing window typically provides bright or high light. Plants in a north-facing window get low light, whereas those in an east or west window receive medium light. Among other variables, the intensity of light changes with the seasons and drops as you move away from the window. In summer, for instance, plants grow as well a few feet away from a window as they do sitting on the windowsill in winter.

Plants will show you if they're getting too much light (burned or bleached leaves) or not enough (spindly stems, pale leaves, leaves drop off). Peace lily *(Spathiphyllum)* and Chinese evergreen *(Aglaonema)* are two of the best foliage plants to grow in low light.

"WATCH FOR BEAUTIFUL LIGHT in your home. These are precisely the places plants will grow. Plants can't grow in dark corners. And what is the point if they can't be seen and appreciated?"

—Peter Strauss

Rescued from the dumpsters of time, architectural pieces like this one bring an aura of mystery to the garden.

Sculpture in the Garden

Imagine discovering ancient ruins in your garden. The effect will be real, even if the circumstance is not, when you place sculpture among the plants.

You may not think of yourself as an artist, but when you plant art in the garden, your work shines in its own gallery. Place one substantial piece, such as concrete architectural salvage, in a way that makes it appear as though it's been there for ages. You'll create a pleasing sense of discovery as well as an artful effect.

A piece of sculpture in the garden provides a unique, enjoyable focal point. Wedge a massive work of art into the soil at a curious angle and see how it arrests the eye. Whether you nestle an abstract form or a graceful figure between the foliage and flowers, it acts as a powerful ornament that brings focus to the plants. You can rescue vintage building materials from old buildings that have been demolished and give them new life in your yard.

Depending on the size and construction, a sculpture adds structure, dimension, color, and the unexpected to the setting. Concrete or stone pieces suggest age and substance, and they typically stand up to harsh environments. Copper, bronze, or other metal pieces develop character-rich patinas when left to weather outdoors. Wood boasts an earthiness that blends with most gardens but has to be protected from the elements. All sculpture adds distinction in the winter months.

▲ **What Is That I See?**
In the context of the larger garden picture, architectural salvage catches the eye and creates a sense of mystery that draws you in.

Materials and Equipment

- Concrete architectural salvage, such as a piece of cornice, broken column, or large urn (use any large piece of sculpture or ornament that appears weathered and ancient)

The Plants
shown on the opposite page

- One 8" feather reed grass (*Calamagrostis* × *acutiflora* 'Karl Foerster')
- One 10" variegated red-twig dogwood (*Cornus alba* 'Elegantissima')
- One 6" false sunflower (*Heliopsis*)
- One 3" chartreuse coleus
- Six 3" groundcovers, such as *Sedum acre* and creeping thyme

▲ **Edging Creates Order**
Install an edging between the lawn and the garden bed. This keeps grass where it belongs and gives the plantings definition. Set the edging slightly above soil level.

Plan of Action

1 Explore architectural salvage suppliers to find a piece of sculpture. Check your phone book or the Internet for a list of nearby salvagers.

2 Place sculpture on a stable foundation away from foot traffic, sprinklers, and mowers. Where repeated freezing and thawing pose potential damage, display the piece off the ground on a base or platform.

3 Aim for artful effects when planting around the sculpture. Include one or two favorite plants nearby to highlight them. Choose an ornamental grass that waves gently in breezes as a plant companion. Plant a simple palette of one or two groundcovers, such as *Sedum acre* or creeping thyme, at the base.

Ornamental Grasses

A MAIDEN GRASS comes in many species and varieties, mostly vigorous and tall (4 to 6 feet). Once established, it is tolerant of wet and dry conditions. Grow it in full sun. Hardy in Zones 4 to 10.

B FOUNTAIN GRASS forms neat mounds 1 to 3 feet tall in rich, moist, well-drained soil; site it in sun or light shade. Hardy in Zones 5 to 9.

C JAPANESE BLOOD GRASS is valued for its coloration—fresh green at the base and flaming red blades in fall. Give it sun to part shade and moist soil. It's best in Zones 4 and 5 where the seeds won't ripen and sprout into all-green weeds the next year. Hardy in Zones 4–10.

D BLACK MONDO GRASS is not a true grass but a grasslike lily relative with unusual, nearly black leaves. Best for sun to part shade and moist soil; for edging and for pots. Hardy in Zones 6–10.

E TUFTED HAIR GRASS is a smaller, very refined grass that produces airy clouds of golden seedheads above mounds of fine-textured leaves. It needs sun and moist soil. Hardy in Zones 4–9.

Ornamental grasses work beautifully in combinations and as edgings, groundcovers, or screens. Many perennial grasses withstand tough conditions. Clumping-type grasses form neat mounds. Running-type grasses spread by underground stems, becoming invasive. Use runners as erosion-controlling groundcovers. Otherwise, keep runners in a container, then plant them, pot and all, in the garden. Grasses remain good-looking through fall and winter. Leave foliage on plants to help protect them over winter. In early spring, before the plants resume growth, cut the browned blades to 4 to 6 inches and give plants their annual feeding of a slow-release, all-purpose plant food. Water new plantings regularly the first season. Established plants do well with occasional rain, but you must water deeply during drought. After several years in the garden, if a plant begins to die in the center, divide it. Dig it up in early spring, split the old plant into several new ones, and replant them.

A *Miscanthus sinensis* 'Rotsilber'

B *Pennisetum alopecuroides* 'Moudry'

C *Imperata cylindrica* 'Red Baron'

D *Ophiopogon planiscapis* 'Nigrescens' with branch of *Acer palmatum* in fall.

E *Deschampsia caespitosa* 'Goldschleier'

Edging Between Lawn and Beds

INSTALLING PLASTIC EDGING

1 Rent a bedding edger to make fast work of edging with steel, plastic, or stone. There is even a blade for installing invisible fencing for your dog!

2 After using the bedding edger, it's almost child's play to install a plastic edging between lawn and flower bed. Fill in with soil and top with about 2 inches of mulch.

GARDEN EDGING MAKES BEDS look neater, it helps keep out weeds and grass where you don't want them, and it saves time spent on maintenance. Placing a band of ground-level bricks around a bed provides a path for a lawn mower's wheels, making mowing easier. Otherwise, you could spend hours hand trimming the lawn edges.

1 Cut a clean edge around the bed, using a spade or an edging tool. Dig a trench along the edge that's as deep and wide as a brick. Choose a color of brick that suits your garden.

2 To determine the number of bricks you will need to edge the garden, measure the perimeter of the bed and divide that number by the length of a brick (usually 8 inches). Lay the bricks in place end to end as shown.

3 Backfill with soil, then apply a mulch right up to the bricks. This simple treatment adds immeasurably to the satisfaction of grooming a lawn and flower border and makes the yard look shipshape.

> **"EDGING LAWNS AND GARDEN BEDS** is practical and beautiful, too. Besides bender board and plastic edger, consider using bricks, tiles, gravel, or mulch."
> —Peter Strauss

Framing a View Through a Side Yard

A sunny, inviting corridor flanked by apple trees and roses replaces a side yard that once was nothing more than an out-of-the-way place.

▲ Create a Focal Point
A Victorian urn planted with angel-wing begonias, caladiums, and variegated ivy is displayed on a blue pedestal. The wood-framed screen with white vinyl privacy lattice emphasizes the urn.

▲ Roses All Season
The 'Flower Carpet' roses come into bloom in late spring or early summer and continue nonstop (or in waves) until the first killing frost. They require cutting back only once in spring at the beginning of the season. This encourages vigorous new shoots and lots of flowering.

A simple lattice arch and rows of colonnade apple trees transform a small, south-facing side yard into an elegant, sheltered alley. The elements combine pleasantly, leading your eyes and feet to the backyard.

A view may be particularly aesthetic or mostly practical, as long as you plan for it and include a focal point. In this case, an antique clay pot on a matching pedestal draws you in. The view could be a couple of lawn chairs deftly placed in the distance or an old wheelbarrow planted with flowers.

An ideal garden frame allows only a partial view and thereby provokes a sense of mystery. In the setting shown, a lattice arch at the side yard entry frames the view and constitutes a standing invitation to enter the garden and see what lies beyond the field of vision.

The simple-but-defined sense of order that arises from the formal design gives the small space clarity and impact. The neat, evenly spaced trees and dense rose hedging create a rhythm of repeated elements that paces your passage until you reach the destination: a beautiful backyard garden. The plantings are unexpected in a side yard, which is usually left to plain lawn or mulch and a few shrubs.

Materials and Equipment

- 1×8 cedar or other rot-resistant wood to raise the planting beds on either side of the walkway
- 1×2 wood stakes to secure boards in place for raised planting beds

The Plants
shown on the opposite page

- 30 colonnade apple trees, six each of five cultivars: 'ScarletSpire', 'CrimsonSpire', 'EmeraldSpire', 'UltraSpire', and 'Maypole' (flowering crabapple, to pollinate the colonnades)
- 20 'Flower Carpet' roses

Plan of Action

1 Determine the view and focal point you want to frame. Imagine the view from both ends of the corridor.

2 Decide how to frame the entry (with an arbor, a gate, or upright plantings) and what to plant along the corridor (low-maintenance dwarf trees and shrubs are recommended).

3 Place a bench along one side of the corridor, especially if there is a pleasant spot to sit in the shade.

4 Top the pathway with gravel or stepping-stones to reinforce its intention, or concentrate on maintaining a healthy turf walkway.

5 Another way to create a corridor is to line the walkway on either side at 4- to 6-foot intervals with tree-form roses, Korean lilacs, or almost any available plant that has a strongly vertical form. Underplant with a groundcover such as periwinkle, lamium, ajuga, or coral bells.

Typical side yards merely provide breathing room between neighbors. But the space can be transformed into an outdoor destination when it features a defined entrance (in this case an arch), plantings that lead the eyes and the feet forward in a process of discovery, and a focal point in the distance that acts as a kind of magnet.

Columnar Fruit Trees For Small Spaces

A 'SCARLETSPIRE' APPLE is a Colonnade series apple with dark pink to white flowers in spring followed by red-and-green apples in fall. All cultivars of the Colonnade series apple trees are of narrow, columnar form excellent in small spaces.

B 'CRIMSONSPIRE' APPLE is another Colonnade series variety with pink-tinged white flowers in spring and crisp, tangy crimson fruit in fall.

C 'EMERALDSPIRE' APPLE is a Colonnade series apple with pink-blushed white blooms in spring and golden-toned green apples in fall.

D 'ULTRASPIRE' APPLE is a Colonnade that is exceptionally compact in habit and produces green-blushed red fruit in fall. It grows 6 to 8 feet tall and 2 feet across.

E 'MAYPOLE' FLOWERING CRABAPPLE serves as a pollinator for the Colonnade series apples. Dark pink spring blooms precede ornamental crimson-purple crabapples, which the birds appreciate in fall.

If you plant fruit trees in your garden, no matter what their size, you'll reap armloads of luscious fruit and enjoy the trees' beauty through the seasons. Colonnade (columnar form) trees are small enough to live on a deck or a patio in pots (20 inches or larger). In the ground, the mature trees reach 8 to 15 feet tall and 20 to 24 inches wide. Most apple trees require cross-pollination from another variety in order to produce fruit; the columnar Maypole flowering crabapple makes an excellent pollinator for any of the edible Colonnade series apple varieties. Plant these tall, slender sentinel trees along a wall or a fence, or use them to flank an entry in a location with at least six to eight hours of sun and well-drained soil. The Colonnades are cold-hardy in Zones 4 to 8 and need a winter chill to grow successfully. If you live in the Deep South or another warm-winter area, ask your local extension service for a list of appropriate fruit trees.

Malus 'Scarletspire'

Malus 'Crimsonspire'

Malus 'Emeraldspire'

Malus 'Ultraspire'

Malus 'Maypole'

Planting a Tree or Shrub

PLANT A TREE OR SHRUB in early spring or early fall so the plant has time to begin rooting and growing before it faces stressful weather. Choose a site that has the right soil and light, and enough room for the plant to reach mature size.

1 Dig a planting hole about twice as wide and about the same depth as the plant's root ball. Use the handle of a shovel or broom to determine the correct planting depth. Try not to disturb soil in the bottom of the hole.

2 If you are planting a container-grown plant, tip the tree or shrub and remove the container. Using a hose, spray the root ball to moisten the soil and loosen some of the outer roots.

3 Position the root ball in the hole, aligning the top with ground level. Untie and remove twine or fabric from balled-and-burlapped plants. Loosen soil around sides of hole to encourage roots to spread into the existing soil.

4 Backfill around the root ball with soil enriched with up to 50 percent of an amendment high in organic matter such as packaged garden soil. When the hole is half full, water well. Finish filling the hole with soil. Mound soil to create a basin around the plant to catch rainwater and facilitate irrigation. Water again.

5 Apply mulch 2 to 4 inches thick. Continue to feed throughout the first one to five years after planting.

"MOST NEWLY PLANTED TREES SHOULD NOT BE STAKED. Some movement from wind encourages the trunk to develop more strength. However, if a tree is top-heavy with dense foliage (as are some evergreens), staking it through its first season helps protect the tree from wind until it is established."

—Peter Strauss

An old beverage-bottle case from a flea market finds a new life as the vertical home for burro's-tail sedums and ghost plant *(Graptopetalums),* easy-care succulents that always look great.

Hang Your Garden On a Wall

No room to garden? Not a problem! Turn an old wooden soda-pop case into an instant living sculpture—a vertical garden on a wall.

Succulents (water-storing plants) are an astonishing group that merits broad use. Most hail from desert or semidesert areas of the world, so they're well-adjusted to hot, dry climates. As garden plants, they represent a diverse group that looks good year-round. They are dramatic but not demanding.

Choose from among dozens of groups of succulents, including sedum, hen and chicks, aloe, jade, and wax plants. Most feature fleshy leaves or stems in sculptural forms and fascinating textures. Many show off delightful flowers and have humorous names, such as hen and chicks (*Sempervivum*) or a sedum

called pork and beans.

The boxed garden shown on this and the opposite page includes two plant varieties, but your collection could be more varied. Hang the display on a fence or wall where you will see it often.

Succulents do need water, but you must avoid overwatering. Allow the moss to dry between weekly drenchings. Let the box sit and drain before hanging it back up. Feed two or three times a year using all-purpose water-soluble plant food at the rate of ¼ teaspoon per gallon. Unless you live in a desert climate, move the box indoors for the winter. Succulents make good houseplants in a sunny place.

Materials and Equipment

- Vintage wooden soda-pop case
- One bag long-strand sphagnum moss
- Bucket of water
- Watering can

The Plants
shown on the opposite page

- Twelve 3" ghost plants (*Graptopetalum paraguayense*)
- Twelve 3" burro's tail (*Sedum morganianum*)

Plan of Action

1 Find a vintage wooden soda-pop case at an antiques store, flea market, or yard sale (or maybe stashed away in your garage).
2 Soak the moss in a bucket of water. Grab a handful of moss and squeeze out the excess water as you prepare to plant the box.
3 Place a small handful of wet moss in the bottom of each of the box's compartments.
4 Remove a plant from its nursery pot and shake any extraneous potting mix off the roots. Wrap the roots in a small handful of wet sphagnum moss. Stuff the moss-wrapped root mass into a compartment. Tuck in additional wet moss to secure the plant in place.
5 Let the box sit and settle for two weeks before hanging it up for display. This allows the plants to begin rooting in place.

▲**Feather the Nest**
Line the bottom of each compartment with wet, long-strand sphagnum moss.

▲**Wrap the Root Balls**
Gently wrap the roots of each plant with a small handful of moistened, long-strand sphagnum moss.

▲**Water Just a Little**
Take down the box to water it weekly or when the moss feels dry.

Favorite Cacti and Succulents

A BURRO'S TAIL is a frost-sensitive member of the Sedum family, a silvery succulent trailer for high light to full sun. Water to maintain soil between moist and on the dry side. Handle carefully so as not to dislodge the leaves.

B GHOST PLANT is a succulent that needs lots of sun and soil that's between moist and quite dry. Move to a frost-free place for winter. Outstanding for silvery, ghostly effects.

C ALOE VERA has fleshy leaves that contain a gel that soothes burns and insect bites. This succulent grows in nearly any light, from shade to full sun. Keep warm. Water to keep soil between moist and on the dry side.

D MAMMILLARIA are small cacti that are easy to grow and fun to cultivate in a collection of different pots. They need full sun in summer and ample water; in winter, protect plants from frost and keep them quite dry.

E PRICKLY PEAR is a large group of cacti, many of which are able to withstand extreme winter cold as well as drought. They all produce astoundingly beautiful flowers in early summer following spring rains.

CACTI AND SUCCULENTS encompass a broad, loose category of plants that have well-developed survival skills. They thrive in the warm, dry air of many homes and offices, thanks to their thick, fleshy leaves or stems that store water. Among thousands of varieties, common cacti and succulents grow easily in a sunny window or a sandy garden. The following list represents a few good plants to start with: barrel cactus (a slow-growing, ball-shaped plant with ferocious thorns); golden ball cactus (round and squat with golden thorns); crown cactus (tight clusters of tiny balls stay compact); Peruvian old man (an upright cactus covered with fine white hair); jade plant (a succulent that resembles a small tree with thick leaves); *Haworthia* (many succulent species with spiky leaves that resist cold); *Lithops* (living stones); *Agave* (slow-growing succulents with spreading rosettes); and string-of-beads plant (a striking trailing succulent with leaves like beads).

Sedum morganianum

Graptopetalum paraguayense

Aloe vera

Mammillaria elongata 'Irish Red'

Opuntia species (cholla, prickly pear, and bunny ears)

Caring for Cacti and Succulents

◀ A dish garden ▶ is a good-looking way to display a collection of cacti. When transplanting, wear heavy gloves and wrap a rolled sheet of newspaper around the plant.

▲ For easy transport and stability against wind, display cacti in this simple-to-make wooden grid.

▲ With wood glue, attach seven 1×2s 14 inches long in the grid pattern shown. Insert screws through ¼" holes drilled in the bottom of the grid and into the drain hole of each pot.

▲ You know you've watered well when water drains out the bottom of the pot. Never leave cacti standing in water.

▲ When transplanting, use a porous potting mix labeled for cacti. It includes large amounts of sand and grit.

Growing cacti and other succulents entails no secret methods. They thrive in warm, dry conditions with sandy soil and occasional soakings.

Grow cacti and succulents in premium, specialty potting mix labeled for cacti. Such potting mixes are porous and drain freely due to their blend of sand, perlite, and potting soil. Use a clay pot slightly larger than the plant; it must have a drainage hole. Repot plants every few years. When handling cacti, protect yourself as shown above.

Indoors, cacti like as much sun as possible. Grow in high light (a south-facing window is preferred; an unobstructed west exposure is second best; a sunny east window is third choice). In summer, take them outdoors and provide a little shade.

Overwatering will rot the roots of cacti, so let the soil dry between waterings. In summer, plants dry out more quickly. Check pots weekly and water thoroughly as needed. Do not let plants sit in water. From fall until late winter, water just enough to keep the plant from shriveling, every two to three weeks.

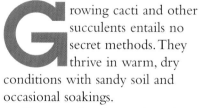

"CACTI WITH SPINES tend to be plants that thrive in sunlight; cacti without spines and most succulents can tolerate some shade. Epiphyllums, or holiday cacti, actually prefer part shade."

—Peter Strauss

Small-Space Solution: Go Vertical

A tower with five levels of flowering takes little more than a square foot of space, yet the visual rewards are obvious. Plant in a morning, enjoy for months.

▲ Position the Bottom Pot First
Assemble the materials, equipment, and plants. Fill the biggest pot with potting mix and tamp it level. Insert a dowel into the soil, centered on the drain hole.

▲ Stack Smaller Pots by Size
Position progressively smaller pots with the dowel through the drain holes, then fill with potting mix and tamp the tops level.

▲ Set the Star Players in Place
Plant three *Calibrachoa*, evenly spaced, in the top pot. Tuck them into the exposed soil around the other pots, leaving 2 to 3 inches between each plant.

Small is beautiful, especially if it means turning a yard challenge into an asset. The entrance you use most for your home, not necessarily the front door, could be an ideal spot for this beauty treatment. It's easy, it's different, and it uses common materials for an uncommon effect.

The unusual container towers take advantage of vertical space and accentuate the porch and steps with the vibrant flowers of cascading *Calibrachoa*, a compact plant that blooms profusely from spring through late fall. Help the plants thrive by watering the towers regularly. *Calibrachoa* prefers moist soil, so water the plants daily during hot weather. Feed regularly with all-purpose plant food.

Build each tower in place, starting with the largest pot and filling it with potting mix. Stand the dowel in the potting mix and slide the next-smaller-size pot over the dowel. Set the container on top of the filled pot beneath it. Fill the second pot with potting mix. Repeat the steps until the tower is complete.

After the killing frost, you can remove all the *Calibrachoa* plants and in their place insert evergreen cuttings to give the towers a lively appearance through the winter.

Materials and Equipment
(for two plant towers)

- Two 14" clay pots
- Two 12" clay pots
- Two 10" clay pots
- Two 8" clay pots
- Two 6" clay pots
- Two ½" wood dowels 36" long
- One 2-cubic-foot bag of potting mix

The Plants
shown on the opposite page

- One flat of *Calibrachoa* 'Cherry Pink'
- One flat of *Calibrachoa* 'Trailing Blue'

Plan of Action

1 Select any site for the living pot tower where there is sunlight for a half day or more. You can use impatiens if the ideal spot is more shady than sunny.
2 Start with the biggest pot and place it where you want the tower to grow. Fill with potting soil, tamp down, and level the surface. Insert the wood dowel through the soil, centering it on the drain hole. If the pot is placed directly on the ground, you can drive the wood down through the hole and several inches into the soil to give it more stability.
3 Add the next size pot, threading it through the drain hole and onto the dowel. Fill with potting soil. Continue until the top pot is positioned and filled.
4 Set *Calibrachoa* plants all around, mixing and matching the colors as you like.
5 Repeat with the second set of pots and place them in the garden as accents.

It's hard to imagine a place where two simple plantings could have more of an impact than on either side of the front steps. Common clay pots and two colors of *Calibrachoa*, a petunia cousin, have a magical effect all summer until the first hard frost.

Cascading, Spilling Flowers

A CALIBRACHOA is an annual that resembles a pint-size petunia. It blooms all summer in sun to half sun and moist soil, with regular feedings of all-purpose plant food. It's ideal in baskets or window boxes.

B BALCONY GERANIUMS are annuals that thrive in sun to half sun, with moist to slightly dry soil and regular applications of all-purpose plant food. They provide nonstop bloom for baskets and window boxes. Pinch off spent blooms.

C FUCHSIA needs cool shade in hot climates (more sun in cool climates), plus moist soil and feedings with water-soluble plant food for acid-loving plants. Ideal for baskets, the dangling flowers are a beacon to hummingbirds. Hardy in Zones 10–11.

D TRAILING SNAPDRAGONS are annuals that bloom nonstop from spring to fall but do best in cooler weather. Routine deadheading promotes bloom. Provide sun to half sun; keep moist and feed regularly with all-purpose plant food.

E TRAILING VERBENA produces vivid flowers on densely branching, trailing plants that are heat-tolerant. Provide half to full sun and moist soil. Feed regularly with all-purpose plant food. This plant is lovely as a groundcover, in baskets, or spilling from any container. Hardy in Zones 6–11; often grown as an annual.

PLANTS HAVE HABITS TOO. The way they grow and the overall form they take (upright, prostrate, weeping) provide you with clues as to where and how to grow them. Take advantage of some plants' proclivity for trailing and cascading, for example. They spill out of beds and containers, softening edges and adding interest to the scene via their tumbling antics. Cascading plants lend an air of casual beauty to hanging baskets, window boxes, and patio or deck planters. It's possible to accomplish the effect of a hanging basket anywhere in the garden; simply plant these beauties in a container of any sort and stage them on a wall, step, or tree stump. To highlight cascading plants, use just one variety in a hanging basket. Or combine trailers and plants with different habits, some upright and some spreading, for layers of color and texture. When combining different plants, plant the trailers around the edge of the container for best effect.

Calibrachoa 'Trailing Pink'

Pelargonium peltatum

Fuchsia 'Swingtime'

Antirrhinum 'Luminaire'

Verbena 'Silver Anne'

Catching Plant Problems Early

▲ Leaves with webs and yellow or gray speckles may have spider mites. Shake a leaf over white paper; if specks move, treat for mites.

◄ Before you take steps to remedy a pest or disease, identify it correctly. A magnifying glass can be a big help. Here, the problem appears to be mealybug, an insect that feeds on plant sap.

▲ Sticky honeydew on the surfaces of leaves indicates the presence of insects. Look for scale or aphids.

▲ Brown scale matures as a raised bump; early on, the insects are pale and smaller.

An ounce of prevention truly pays off when it comes to all plants, and it is doubly important in small spaces. The healthier a plant, the more able it is to resist pests and diseases. Giving plants what they need in terms of light, soil, water, and food is the key to their success. Sometimes problems arise due to one of these elements, be it too much or too little.

First, identify the problem. If you notice wilted leaves on a plant, consider the possibilities: Does the soil feel dry? Is the plant getting too much sun? Has it outgrown its pot? Are there any signs that indicate disease? Distinguishing between a cultural problem and a pest or disease is half the solution. Look closely at your plants. Stop to smell the roses and check their health in

▲ When you take a daily stroll through the garden, keep an eye out for emerging problems and focus on preventing their development as soon as possible.

the process. You'll soon recognize the difference between a healthy plant and one that needs help. When you water, watch for signs of insect problems and choose the mildest remedies first: Pick off insects, then spray with a solution of soapy water; if there are lots of bugs, prune the affected area, then spray.

"THE ORTHO HOME GARDENERS' PROBLEM SOLVER is my favorite aid for identifying and solving plant problems. This is a book that covers it all."

—Peter Strauss

A half-sunny window is the ideal place to grow and show orchids. Grouping several in a shallow basket hides the different growing pots and helps create a pocket of moist air around them. Another option is to set the pots directly on a surface of pebbles placed about an inch deep in a waterproof tray.

Easy Orchid Window Garden

Space-age propagation techniques, low-cost production, and ready availability have made orchids today's most popular flowering houseplants.

Nature has given us thousands of orchids, variously able to withstand temperatures from the tundra to the tropics. Today's orchids are remarkably easy to grow, and many are sold for reasonable prices in home centers and nurseries. When shopping for orchids, buy three or four. Grouping several orchids together is easier than growing only one, because multiple plants create a higher moisture content in the air around them.

You can encourage new growth and blooms when the last flower fades by cutting off the flowering stem to the base. If your plant is a *Phalaenopsis,* look for signs of secondary spikes before cutting the old stem. If detected, cut off the old stem directly above the new shoot. If not, try to force a secondary shoot: Cut off the old stem directly above the second node (slightly swollen place) from the base.

Orchid plants do well in the same bright-to-sunny window gardens and similar temperatures as African violets, begonias, geraniums, and ferns. Place pots on top of pebbles in a humidity tray kept filled with water to help give them the moist air they need in order to thrive. Apply orchid plant food weekly at quarter strength and repot yearly (see page 105).

▲ Watering
Once or twice a week, run tepid water through the pot; drain the pots in the sink, then return to the display. Never leave an orchid standing in water.

▲ Summering
When temperatures are warm enough to grow tomatoes outdoors, place orchids outdoors in a plastic-mesh crate in part sun, part shade. Shower them every other day or so unless it rains. Feed once a week at quarter strength.

Materials and Equipment
- Humidity tray (waterproof and 1–2" deep)
- Plastic sheeting to line tray
- Sandstone pebbles to fill tray
- Slender bamboo canes
- Raffia for tying orchid to cane
- Two 5-inch-deep woven baskets
- Orchid plant food (30-10-10)

The Plants
shown on the opposite page
- One *Oncidium* hybrid
- Three *Paphiopedilum* hybrids with silver-mottled leaves
- One *Dendrobium* 'Emerald Fantasy'
- One *Phragmipedium* hybrid
- Five *Phalaenopsis* hybrids

▲ Humidifying
Use a waterproof tray about an inch deep. Fill with clean pebbles. Add water as needed to maintain at a level just below the bottom of the pots.

Plan of Action
1 To make the baskets waterproof, line them with plastic sheeting or position a plastic saucer to fit under each plant's pot.
2 Arrange individual orchid plants so the leaves stand free of one another and all the flowers show off their individual beauty.
3 Insert a slender bamboo cane beside each flower spike; tie the spike in place with raffia so it stands gracefully but also sits well in relation to the others.
4 Set the baskets in a place that has light and temperatures comfortable for sitting and reading or doing needlework.
5 Every three or four days, take the baskets to a sink and in turn remove each orchid plant and run tepid water across the surface of the growing mix; allow excess water to drain, then return the plants to their position on the tray.

Easiest Orchids

A PANSY ORCHID, known as *Miltonia* and *Miltoniopsis*, thrives in temperatures around 55 to 75°F and in moist, circulating air.

B MOTH ORCHID, or *Phalaenopsis*, blooms for months on end in bright light, not direct sun, and temperatures comfortable for humans, basically a range between 60 and 80°F.

C DENDROBIUM has cane-like stems topped by arching sprays of incredibly long-lasting flowers. Blooms last longer in bright light but new growth needs some direct sun to mature and bloom; 60 to 80°F.

D CYMBIDIUM grows in bright light to some direct sun, outdoors in summer if possible. Do not bring inside until there is a chill, about 40°F, which sets the new flower buds.

E DANCING LADY, or *Oncidium*, needs strong light in summer. When indoors, keep in temperatures of 55 to 80°F, with fresh, moist, moving air.

Orchids are the most rapidly changing group of flowering plants today, in part because they so readily can be crossed to create new genera, but also because they respond so favorably to multiplication by new high-tech cloning techniques. This means that more beautiful, longer-lasting, more easily cultivated orchids are constantly reaching the market at surprisingly low prices.

The orchids pictured here and on page 102 are among the best for beginners. They are also among those you are most likely to find at your local nursery, florist, or garden center. *Oncidium, Dendrobium,* and *Cymbidium* are suited to sunnier indoor gardens, whereas *Phalaenopsis, Paphiopedilum, Phragmipedium, Miltonia,* and *Miltoniopsis* thrive in bright reflected light out of hot direct sunlight. All of them thrive in pleasantly moist air that circulates freely.

Miltonia 'Maurice Powers'

Phalaenopsis 'KB's Happy Camper'

Dendrobium 'Orchid Acres Stephanie'

Cymbidium ultimatum 'Santa Barbara'

Oncidium 'Kathleen'

Repotting Orchids

▲ The glazed ceramic pots shown above have holes cut in the sides to suit the needs of air, or epiphytic, plants such as orchids. The holes let moisture and fresh air reach the roots. Unglazed clay or terra-cotta pots also are available with drainage cuts in the sides of the pots, in addition to the conventional bottom drain hole. Most of the showy orchids grown as houseplants are epiphytic in nature and grow only in a medium labeled specifically for orchids. They cannot grow in ordinary garden soil, no matter what additives are used.

MOTH ORCHIDS and other orchid plants in general need to be repotted before the potting mix in which they are growing (usually a chunky bark medium) starts to decompose. This usually occurs about once a year.

1 This young moth orchid has outgrown its 3-inch plastic pot; its thrifty roots are growing outside the confines of the pot.

2 Remove the old pot and every last bit of the old potting mix. Orchids do not grow well in old potting mix, no matter how much you feed and water. Clip off any roots that are dead, shriveled, or broken.

3 Position the plant in the center of a clean, fresh pot, such as this glazed ceramic pot designed for epiphytic (air-growing) orchids. It has air and drainage holes cut in the sides. Fill in around the roots with a potting mix labeled specifically for orchids. Add about 2 cups of water to the bag of fresh mix to premoisten it. Knead the bag and leave the mix to soak overnight. Then drain and use.

4 Water the transplanted orchid by applying room-temperature water all across the surface of the potting mix. Allow to drain. If water remains in a leaf cup, blot it out with a piece of paper towel.

"WATCH FOR A NEW BUD on a *Phalaenopsis* flower spike. When the older part finishes blooming, cut off the stalk above the secondary bud. Or cut off the old stem just above the second node or swelling from its base."

—Peter Strauss

Growing Cut Flowers Indoors

Amaryllis bulbs make splendid gifts. Nature neatly packaged them with a glorious surprise inside. Pot up to a dozen in one big pot as a perennial treat for yourself.

▲ **Efficiency in Numbers**
A dozen amaryllis bulbs set in an 18-inch pot can spend the summer outdoors, storing up energy to bloom profusely indoors during the dead of winter.

▲ **Bold Leaves for the Summer**
Grouped in a roomy ceramic pot, the amaryllis bulbs and foliage support each other and boast a tropical look, unlike a single bulb with floppy leaves.

A single amaryllis bloom brings beauty to any room in winter. Imagine what a dozen blooming all at once can do! Few gardeners realize that amaryllis flowers actually last longer when cut. When bulbs are massed in a large pot, you can harvest stem after stem of gorgeous cut flowers for weeks.

Mix or match varieties in your group planting. Amaryllis come in an astonishing range of colors: white, pink, peach, red, and yellow. Choose from miniatures, doubles, and mini doubles, bold stripes, and subtle edgings.

Follow these steps to keep your cut-flower "factory" in production:

After you've enjoyed the last of the cut flowers, set the pot of bulbs in a warm, sunny spot. Water when the soil feels dry. Feed once or twice a month using a tomato plant food from the beginning of new leaf growth until Labor Day. Put the pot outside in full to half sun when spring warms up. In early fall, stop watering and feeding. Bring the pot indoors before frost and set it in a dark, cool place (60°F), such as the basement, for eight to 12 weeks of rest. Remove foliage only after it turns yellow and dies down. In early winter, move the pot to a sunny, warm spot and resume watering and feeding. The fast-growing flower buds and leaves will soon appear.

Materials and Equipment

- One 18" pot or bowl
- One 1-cubic-foot bag of all-purpose premium potting mix

The Plants
shown on the opposite page

- Twelve amaryllis bulbs, mixed or matched

Plan of Action

1 Start bulbs in fall. Position them 1 to 2 inches apart, snuggling each into the surface of the potting soil and covering with more soil so the upper half to one-third of the bulb remains exposed. Water well.

2 Set in a sunny, warm place and water sparingly, if at all, until signs of growth are apparent: You'll see fat buds poking up alongside green leaf tips.

3 As growth becomes active, water a little more, but do not leave the pot standing in water. Water and feed regularly.

4 If you don't use them as cut flowers, remove each flowering stalk at the base as it finishes. When the weather is warm enough to plant tomatoes, take the amaryllis pot outdoors. Feed and water as described in the text above.

5 Before frost, bring the pot indoors and allow it to dry out (see text above). As the new flowering season begins, enjoy the blooms en masse or cut them and place all around the house in vases of water.

The amazing thing about amaryllis is that the flowers seem to last even longer cut and in a beautiful bouquet than when they are left on the plant. The bulbs can be brought to bloom in any convenient spot that is bright and warm. Cut the flower stalks as the buds begin to open and plunge them in cool water.

Favorite Bulbs for Indoor Blooms

A PAPERWHITE NARCISSUS gives heady fragrance and blooms easily without special chilling. Set bulbs in a pot of soil or in a dish with pebbles and enough water to reach the bottom of the bulbs.

B HYACINTH bulbs can be kept in a paper bag in the refrigerator vegetable crisper or similar cool place for up to 14 weeks, then placed in a glass to begin the forcing process (see text at right).

C CALLA LILY grows best indoors in a warm place with lots of sun. As tender tropicals, they don't require chilling. Set the tuber (bulblike root structure) in a pot of moist soil. When growth becomes active, leave the pot standing in a saucer of water. Feed with all-purpose plant food.

D EASTER LILY purchased in bloom can be set in the garden after flowering, with the bulb planted about 6 inches deep. It may bloom as early as the following summer. Hardy in Zone 5.

E CLIVIA is a subtropical evergreen. Grow outdoors in warm weather in a spot with bright indirect light. Water and feed freely. In winter, bring it indoors before the first frost and keep it cool and on the dry side.

FLOWERING BULBS GROWN INDOORS prove that you can fool Mother Nature. You can coax hardy spring-flowering bulbs such as tulips and daffodils, which are ordinarily planted in the garden in fall, into blooming indoors during winter. The growing technique, called forcing, mimics nature's seasonal cycle as you chill potted bulbs at 35 to 48°F for at least 14 weeks in a refrigerator or an unheated garage. Keep the soil evenly moist; drying out after the roots begin is a main cause of failure. Chill the bulbs away from ripe apples, or they won't develop properly. Then move the bulbs to a cool (55 to 60°F), sunny room or windowsill and watch the leaves, then the flowers, develop. If you force more than one pot of bulbs, bring them out of chilling one at a time to stagger their blooms and enjoy them for weeks on end. Look for bulbs labeled "prechilled" to plant in time for blooms as early as the holidays.

A

Narcissus (paperwhite)

B

Hyacinthus orientalis

C

Zantedeschia rehmannii violacea 'California Calla'

D

Lilium longiflorum

E

Clivia miniata

Planting and Growing Tender Bulbs in a Container

Tender bulbs cannot survive freezing winter conditions in the garden, so you must dig them, store them indoors over winter, and replant them in the garden come spring. But there's a much easier way: Plant them in portable gardens. When you plant tender bulbs, such as calla lilies, caladiums, Peruvian daffodils, dahlias, and tuberous begonias, in containers, you can enjoy them in the summer garden, then move them indoors—pot and all—when they have finished blooming as fall rolls around. Keep the potted bulbs in a cool, dry place, such as the basement, or on shelving in an unheated but frost-free garage or other outbuilding. Once the foliage

▲ Paperwhite narcissus bulbs can be started at intervals from early fall to mid winter for bloom in three to six weeks. Use a waterproof bowl (nonporous, without drain holes). Add a cushion of potting mix in the bottom. Snuggle the narcissus bulb bases into the mix. Cover with pebbles until just the tips show. Add water. Keep cool (40 to 60°F) in bright light for best bloom.

has browned and dried, cut it to soil level. In spring, when the garden begins flowering, it's time to bring the pots out of hibernation. Set the pots outdoors in their preferred location: sun or shade. Begin watering as needed (in the absence of rain). Feed as you water with a hose-end sprayer, or mix all-purpose water-soluble plant food and apply it with a watering can.

"SUMMER YOUR AMARYLLIS OUTDOORS, moving pots to take advantage of seasonal temperatures and light. Apply tomato plant food frequently to promote leaf growth and stronger bulbs for the next year."

—Peter Strauss

In this chapter

112 LIVING HERB CENTERPIECES
Offer delicious herbs and flowers as colorful pick-and-eat centerpieces for an outdoor party.

114 Plants: Ornamental Edibles for Small Containers
115 Technique: Grooming and Deadheading

116 LIGHT UP YOUR PARTY
Your garden party will sparkle with candles reflected in the water of a tiered birdbath fountain that's nestled within cascading plants.

118 Plants: Cascading Foliage Plants
119 Technique: Protecting Transplants from Sun and Wind

120 FROM POTTING BENCH TO PARTY BAR
Turn your potting bench into a lively bar with a little paint and edible tropical flowers growing in pots.

122 Plants: Edible Tropical Flowers
123 Technique: Growing Indoor Plants

124 DOUBLE-DUTY SIX-PACKS
Decorate with blooming annuals in small, showy containers, then transplant them to larger pots or to the garden.

126 Plants: Bedding All-Stars for Summer-Long Color
127 Technique: Planting Bedding Plants

128 THINK BIG WHEN STAGING A PARTY
Big pots and multiples equal maximum impact for your outdoor living area.

130 Plants: Ideal Container Partners
131 Technique: Planting in Big Containers

Gardens That Entertain

Invite friends and family to mingle in the backyard and enjoy the setting as well as one another. Create a cheerful scene that greets guests and makes them feel welcome. Whether you host an impromptu gathering, a casual meal, or a big bash, plants enhance the experience. You can make a centerpiece for the table in minutes using plants your guests can take home; turn a potting bench into a serving sideboard; and put together colorful container gardens for summer-long color, fragrance, and privacy screening. Fresh air, plants, and sunshine (or moonglow) have a way of boosting spirits for any social occasion.

Sweet and savory herbs and flowers combine in decorative centerpieces that dinner guests are invited to snip and use to flavor their food. Above, a bowl holds some of the most aromatic culinary herbs for savory dishes. The dessert-oriented scheme at right includes stevia, an herb that is sweeter than sugar.

Living Herb Centerpieces

Snip-and-eat centerpieces that feature herbs and edible flowers provide fun, flavor, and beauty all in one.

Let fragrant herbs and edible flowers take center stage at your next outdoor gathering. In this scheme, collections of plants fill terra-cotta bowls and make beautiful, edible centerpieces that stimulate the conversation as well as the taste buds.

One bowl contains savory herbs for a luncheon or dinner. In the other, sweet-flavored herbs and edible flowers form a centerpiece destined for nibbling when dessert arrives. As arrangements, they are simple to make and maintain. Plant either or both schemes and use them as often as you like. After dinner move them off the table and onto a sunny patio or deck so they can recover for your next get-together. They should be ready for another event in a week or two.

Provide small scissors as part of each place setting so guests can snip bits of the herbs and flowers to sprinkle on their food. For those who'd rather savor the scents than eat the herbs and flowers, you can scatter colorful, aromatic leaves and petals like confetti on the table. Some herb flowers are tasty too.

The plants shown grow well in a container. Feel free to transfer any of them out of the bowl and into the garden or a larger pot when you decide it's time for a change.

▲ Plant Savory Herbs Together
Include your personal favorites among the savory or culinary herbs. Avoid extremes of wet and dry soil. Feed lightly every other week with all-purpose plant food.

▲ Snipping Does Wonders
When the flowers or tips of the plants are clipped regularly for eating, they reward you with more blooms, more vigorous, bushy growth, and more flavor.

▲ Contrast Different Leaves
Finely cut herb leaves such as dill and fennel make flattering companions for bolder shapes such as mint and sage.

Materials and Equipment
- Two 18" terra-cotta bowls
- Premium all-purpose potting mix

The Plants
shown on the opposite page
- Savory bowl: One plant each of globe basil, chives, marjoram, oregano, rosemary, sage, and thyme. Alternative choices include savory, parsley, chervil, and calendula.
- Sweet bowl: One plant each of pansy, lavender, peppermint, orange mint, stevia, and vanilla grass. Alternatives include calendula, viola, and 'Lemon Gem' marigold.

Plan of Action
1 Plant in spring (in cold climates) and enjoy the planters all summer. Plant anytime in warm climates.
2 Choose a container at least 6 inches deep and 18 inches in diameter.
3 Fill the bowl halfway with potting mix. Remove plants from nursery pots, set in place, and fill in all around with more soil.
4 Water the planter when the surface soil first becomes dry.
5 Snip and clip for seasoning or nibbling, and to promote tidy growth.

Ornamental Edibles
For Small Containers

YOU'LL DISCOVER MANY GOOD REASONS to plant herbs and edible flowers in containers. First of all, pots are portable. You can move an edible centerpiece to the table, the patio, the front porch, or wherever you want to enjoy it. In addition, keeping the plants in a place that's within easy reach helps ensure you will use and enjoy them. Gathering a collection in a container allows you to show off delicately detailed plants that might be lost in the midst of a larger garden. Combining a variety of plants results in an artful display of colors, textures, and shapes. Growing plants in pots also helps you get to know their habits and needs up close. Meet the supersweet herb stevia, for example. A potted garden gives you the opportunity to grow unusual, new, or compact varieties of your favorite edible plants, whether that's the incredibly rounded globes of dwarf bush basil or the latest Johnny-jump-up in any of its recently developed color combinations.

A CHIVES is a hardy perennial, grasslike herb with lavender-pink pompon flowers on 12-inch stems. Leaves and flowers have a mild onion flavor good for salads, soups, sauces, and eggs. Hardy in Zones 3–9

B GLOBE BASIL is a supercompact annual with tiny leaves on dense, multiple-branched plants. It naturally grows in neat, 10-inch ball shapes with little pruning. The leaves and flowers have a peppery taste for salads, pesto sauce, and tomatoes.

C JOHNNY-JUMP-UP (*Viola tricolor*) is an annual with small, pansylike flowers that have a mild, wintergreen-like flavor good for invigorating salads and garnishing meat dishes. Plants do best in cool weather; keep soil moist.

D CALENDULA is also known as pot marigold to herb gardeners. The bright yellow to orange blooms have a piquant to slightly bitter taste and add wake-up color to salads. Calendula is an annual that is easy to start from seeds.

E SWEET VERNAL GRASS has a sweet vanilla flavor and aroma. It is grown for its fragrance and was once used for strewing at church doorways. It is a perennial hardy in Zones 3–10.

Allium schoenoprasum

Ocimum basilicum 'Spicy Globe'

Viola tricolor

Calendula officinalis 'Gitana'

Anthoxanthum odoratum

Grooming and Deadheading

▲ Pick, clip, or snap off blooms such as pansy, daylily, marigold, petunia, and dianthus when they are past their prime. Snap off lilies and daylilies where flowers join the stalk.

▲ Use pruners or floral scissors to deadhead plants with tough stems, such as peonies or daisies.

▲ Many shrubs, such as this spirea, can bloom again if cut back by one-third.

▲ Use edging shears to cut back dianthus and encourage another round of bloom.

▲ In addition to deadheading spent blooms, remove dead leaves to improve appearance.

G rooming plants regularly—cleaning out spent, damaged, or dead flowers, leaves, and stems—is a necessary part of gardening that rewards with tidier, healthier, more productive plants. Removing dead flower heads, or deadheading, helps keep plants blooming and looking good. Do it during daily or weekly strolls through the garden and minimize the prospect of being overwhelmed by the task.

Deadhead spring bulbs when the blooms fade and before seedpods start to appear, but don't remove the leaves until they have fully browned. As the plants slowly wither, the leaves feed and restore the bulbs for next year's flowering.

At the end of the gardening season, groom the garden and remove spent annuals, vegetables, and herbs. Clean up any diseased plant parts to help prevent recurrence next year. Leave ornamental grasses and all but the messiest perennials and vines to help insulate their roots over winter and add some interest in an otherwise bare garden. In early spring, remove the brown leaves and stems.

"DEADHEADING IS FOOLING MOTHER NATURE. We're encouraging more flowers because biologically the plant needs to produce seeds for a new generation."

—Peter Strauss

Light Up Your Party

When the summer sun has set and company is on its way, put on your party shoes and light a few candles. The pretty glow enhances plants and people alike.

▲ **Assemble All the Materials**
Use the tall, 12-inch pot upside down as a base for the large bowl. Then place the smaller 6-inch pot upside down in the bowl (it will be used as a base for the saucer). Plant the large bowl.

▲ **Position the Glazed Saucer**
When the glazed saucer is in place on top of the inverted small pot, add a layer of colorful polished stones or, if you prefer, use charcoal gray moon stones. Add water almost to the brim.

▲ **Light the Candles!**
At party time or when you want to immerse yourself in your garden's nighttime beauty, add several votive candles to the birdbath saucer.

This festive project combines plants and candlelight for entertaining, beautiful results. Depending on the time of day and your mood, it can serve as a birdbath or a lantern.

This birdbath makes imaginative use of clay pots. A selection of bright, cascading plants gives it a lively flair. Birds flock to the planted bath by day, drinking and splashing. By night, it transforms into an elegant lantern, with votive candles in glass holders that sit in the bowl and reflect off the water. Set up the lantern as a centerpiece or an accent. The light will sparkle and lift spirits. Make more than one and enjoy the mood-setting lighting at the edge of a patio, deck, or path.

Planting around the perimeter of the large clay bowl shows off the cascading greenery and gives plants plenty of room to tumble over the edge. Use other cascading plants than the ones listed below, if you wish, especially those that suit an evening garden (see pages 100 and 118). Varieties with silvery foliage, such as artemisia and licorice plant, or white flowers (*Bacopa* and the lighter shades of *Calibrachoa*) come closest to glowing in the dark.

In early fall, recycle the perennial St. Johnswort and dead nettle. Transplant them to a partially shady place in the garden. Water well, and they will return in spring.

Materials and Equipment

- One 11"-diameter, 12"-deep clay pot (base for large bowl)
- One 16"-diameter, 6"-deep clay pot (planted bowl)
- One 3"-diameter, 6"-deep clay pot (base for the glazed saucer)
- One 9"-diameter glazed clay saucer (water-holding bowl)
- One 2-cubic-foot bag of premium potting mix; polished rocks; three votive candles in glass votive cups

The Plants
shown on the opposite page

- Nine 3" Tricolor St. Johnswort (*Hypericum × moseranum* 'Tricolor')
- Nine 3" Beedham's White dead nettles (*Lamium* 'Beedham's White')
- Nine 2" purple lobelias

Plan of Action

1 Turn the 12"×11" clay pot upside down where you want the finished feature to stand.
2 Set the large bowl on top. In the center place the 6"pot upside down and on top of it position the glazed saucer.
3 Half fill the planting bowl with potting soil and position the plants all around. Fill in with more potting soil.
4 Add polished rocks to the glazed saucer.
5 Add candles to make a lantern; remove them to make a birdbath.

This project not only goes together with amazing speed and ease, it shows how ordinary things can be put to different uses for extraordinary effects.

Cascading Foliage Plants

A TRICOLORED ST. JOHNSWORT is valued for its unusual pink, white, and green leaves and trailing habit. It is suited to pots placed in part shade to part sun with plenty of water and good drainage. Hardy in Zones 7–10.

B DEAD NETTLE spreads to become a low carpet of light green leaves with silvery markings, and white, pink, yellow, or purple flowers in spring. It needs rich soil and ample water, and is best with some shade. Hardy in Zones 5–10.

C LICORICE PLANT comes in a range of leaf sizes and colors, from chartreuse to silver to variegated. It grows easily without heavy feeding or watering, and needs at least part sun. Hardy in Zones 10–11.

D 'SILVER FALLS' DICHONDRA, specially bred for containers, is a silver-foliaged, cascading form of a plant commonly used as a lawn substitute or groundcover in Zones 8 to 10.

E ROSEMARY, in its prostrate or trailing form, combines nicely with sun-loving flowering plants or other herbs in pots. Provide at least a half day of full sun, and let the soil dry between waterings. Hardy in Zones 7–10.

WHEN VERDANT FOLIAGE SPRAWLS AND TUMBLES between flowering plants, it serves as a unifying filler and a backdrop. In the garden, trailing plants that root and spread rapidly are usually thought of as groundcovers. The beauty, versatility, and vigor of trailing foliage plants make them an essential component of container plantings, too, on their own or with other flowering plants. The world of foliage extends beyond plain green, venturing into lime, silver, and burgundy.

Plant trailers at the edge of a pot or wall. Place plants 3 to 4 inches apart for fast-filling effects. If trailers get too leggy, trim them back by a third to encourage branching.

Give perennial trailers, such as dead nettle, a second chance after use as container plants. In early fall, transfer them to the garden and water weekly to encourage rooting before winter arrives.

Hypericum × moseranum 'Tricolor'

Lamium maculatum

Helichrysum petiolare 'Rondello'

Dichondra 'Silver Falls'

Rosmarinus officinalis 'Prostratus'

Protecting Transplants From Sun and Wind

Gradually ▶ introduce seedlings or plants grown under lath in a nursery to outdoor life. Set them in a protected place such as under shrubs in the garden for a few days until they acclimate to the outdoors.

▲ Make a protective collar by cutting the bottom out of a heavy-duty 1-gallon nursery pot. Wriggle it into the ground around a young garden plant.

You can plant ▶ warm-weather plants, such as tomatoes, peppers, and melons, earlier when you use an insulating device such as the one shown, available at many garden and home centers. The double wall of plastic holds an insulating layer of water and can be used year after year.

Before putting plants to work in outdoor displays, be sure the tender young ones that have lived only in a greenhouse or in your home have the TLC to make a safe transition to the garden. Protect transplants from sun and wind, especially during the initial weeks of the growing season when weather patterns shift and temperatures fluctuate wildly.

Wind poses a serious threat as it whips and tears at unprotected young plants, sucking moisture from their leaves and the soil. In desert areas, strong winds sandblast plants. Almost any kind of screen or barrier protects plants from wind. Use a temporary shield to block wind but allow light, rain, and air to reach new plantings. Aim for a sturdy, anchored collar, such as a bottomless nursery pot or a milk jug.

Sun ravages tender plants too. They wilt and burn if not hardened off gradually to harsh light and unaccustomed heat. Place seedlings in dappled shade under shrubs, a tree, or an arbor for a few days. You can also drape floating row cover (a lightweight fabric available at most garden and home centers) over plants as a temporary shade that's permeable to rain and air.

"TRANSPLANT AND STAY HOME FOR A FEW DAYS. We tend to transplant on the weekends, then we go off to work for the week. It helps if you can stay around for the first few days to provide proper water and care."

—Peter Strauss

Here's a potting bench that handily does double duty—and more. It's functional for transplanting and other garden chores, but also delightfully painted and easily swept clean for its glamorous second life as a place for serving party fare.

From Potting Bench to Party Bar

Use a potting bench as a hub for outdoor entertaining. You can outfit it to serve up a lively tropical atmosphere as well as food and drinks.

A practical but ordinary potting bench by day becomes party central by night, with a little sleight of hand and a tropical theme. Begin by applying bright paint colors on the wood potting bench.

Set the stage with showy foliage and flowers on and around the potting bench. Aim for big, bold, colorful, and fragrant. More is better. Choose exotic-looking accents, such as gardenia, Chinese hibiscus, bamboo, and palm. Round up plants from indoors as well as outdoors to make a backdrop. Upstage those with colored foliage: canna and croton, along with succulents and bromeliads. A tropical-appearing potted tree (hibiscus or flowering

maple) and a shrub or two (lantana or bougainvillea) provide the scale needed for drama. Fill in with a large fern or a philodendron and pots packed with bright annuals: petunias, marigolds, and zinnias.

Finish the tropical theme with colorful accessories: Tiki torches and hanging lanterns pump up the fun mood, as do calypso or salsa music.

Organize a bar on the potting bench. Include a blender, glasses, an ice bucket, tropical-themed cocktail napkins, lemons, limes, and straws. Tuberous begonias are edible flowers perfect for pick-your-own exotic drink garnishes. Tubs packed with ice cubes, soft drinks, and bottled water refresh and lighten the most sultry of summer evenings.

▲ From Work to Play
A basic potting bench with shelves proves indispensable for gardening and can be tidied up and turned into a sideboard for serving food and drinks.

Materials and Equipment

- Wood potting bench
- Exterior paint in tropical colors
- Lanterns and tiki torches
- Tubs for ice and drinks

The Plants
shown on the opposite page

- Exotic-looking foliage and flowering plants
- Edible tropical flowers, such as hibiscus, jasmine, okra, orange blossom, pineapple guava, pineapple sage, tuberous begonia

▲ A Bloomin' Feast
Serve edible tropical flowers (such as these tuberous begonias) as garnishes for tiki drinks. Nibbling is encouraged, as long as your blooms have been grown without any pest controls.

Plan of Action

1 Dress up a wood potting bench by painting it tropical colors.
2 Add plants to create a setting as pretty and casual as a tropical resort's.
3 Bring on the swizzle sticks, tiny parasols, and other items to stock the bar.
4 Mix up tiki-style cocktails or nonalcoholic drinks using garden-fresh ingredients and edible tropical flower garnishes.
5 Gather friends, bring out the refreshments, turn up the music, and dance!

Edible Tropical Flowers

USE TROPICAL BLOSSOMS as garnishes on icy tropical drinks or home-cooked meals. Savor their beauty, then savor the taste of their petals.

Follow these guidelines to ensure a pleasant flower-eating experience. Not all flowers are edible; some are poisonous. Serve only edible flowers as garnishes. Eat only flowers grown without pesticides. Do not eat flowers from a florist or garden center or those you find by a roadside.

Pick flowers early in the day, after the dew has dried, to capture their peak flavors. Cut them in full bloom and plunge their stems into cool water immediately. Keep flowers in a cool place until serving time. Gently rinse flowers under cool running water. Drain them on a clean cloth. Remove stamens and pistils from the blossoms' centers, keeping the petals intact.

Other edible tropical-appearing flowers include gardenia, jasmine, orange blossom, lemon blossom, hibiscus, banana, ginger, and rose of Sharon.

A NASTURTIUM is an annual that is easy to grow from seed. Choose bush or climbing varieties. Both flowers and leaves have a peppery, watercress flavor. Feed lightly with all-purpose plant food for an abundance of flowers.

B PINEAPPLE SAGE is a tender perennial that grows 3 to 5 feet tall and needs full sun. The scarlet flowers taste sweetly spicy and minty. The leaves smell of pineapple. Hardy in Zones 9–11.

C TUBEROUS BEGONIA grows from a tuber that can't withstand freezing. Grow in a pot and winter indoors. Keep moist and in a mostly shaded spot. The petals have a refreshing crunch and citrus taste.

D YUCCA comes in many species and varieties that are variously cold-hardy. Look for one that is rated for your zone. The plants need full sun and well-drained soil. Eat the sweet petals, not the bitter centers. *Yucca filamentosa* is hardy in Zones 4–9.

E PASSIONFLOWER grows on a vine and, like yucca, comes in various degrees of cold-hardiness. If you eat all the sweet-smelling flowers, you'll miss out on the fruit, which has a delectable tropical taste. Hardy in Zones 8–10.

Tropaeolum majus

Salvia elegans

Begonis × tuberhybrida 'Nonstop Scarlet'

Yucca filamentosa

Passiflora × belotii 'Imperatrice Eugenie'

Growing Indoor Plants

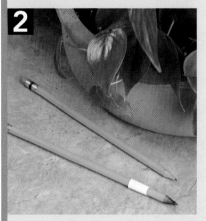

▲ Houseplants with smooth, hard leaves, such as Chinese evergreen (*Aglaonema*, above) and philodendron, benefit from a clean-and-shine spritz. Misting with water benefits bromeliads (below).

CHECK SOIL MOISTURE using an ordinary pencil as a dipstick.

1 Push the lead end of a pencil an inch deep (past the sharpened part of the pencil) into the soil.

2 Pull out the pencil and see if the wood is dark (moist soil) or unaffected (dry soil).

Keep houseplants looking lush and lovely with basic care. Water and food are vital to their health. Amounts and timing depend on plant varieties. Before watering, check soil using the pencil test as shown. Use a long-spout watering can to reach into the pot easily. Pour water until it runs out the bottom of the pot; after a few minutes, empty the pot saucer of excess water. Watch for signs of overwatering, including soft, droopy stems and leaves.

Feed your houseplants recommended quantities of plant food during their main growing season. Sprinkle slow-release pellets on top of the soil, insert plant food spikes, or feed with a liquid or water-soluble plant food every time you water.

Keep plants clean. Bathe plants at least twice a year, placing them in the sink or shower. Remove any yellowing or dead plant parts.

Repot plants at least once a year. Give them more room to grow in a pot that's 2 inches larger in diameter, and replace old depleted soil with fresh new potting mix.

"PLANTS NEED WASHING TOO! Next time you take a shower take your plants in with you! Wash their foliage and let water run through the soil. It cleans their leaves so they breathe easier and leaches out harmful salts."

—Peter Strauss

Double-Duty Six-Packs

In a reversal of the usual garden-to-table scenario, you'll reap the benefits of your favorite bedding plants twice over with this sensible table-to-garden scheme.

▲ **Eat, Drink, and Be Marigold**
Pot up a marigold in a small clay pot with saucer. Add a place card for a dressy table—and encourage guests to keep the plants.

▲ **No Skill Required**
This centerpiece is beautiful, easy, and unusual. The colorful leaves belong to nerve plant (*Fittonia*). Gather small plants on the lower level of a tidbit tray, with pink bonbons above.

▲ **Plant Now and Be Done**
Transplant bedding plants soon after you bring them home, before they become pot-bound and start to decline.

You're in a hurry. Friends are coming over for dinner after work. You barely have time to shop and prepare a meal, let alone tidy up the patio and set the table. Flowers for the table would be the ideal touch, but you just don't have time to arrange flowers.

No problem. Here's a pretty arrangement that's as easy as A–B–C and ready in a flash. The approach adds a cheerful centerpiece to a dining table—and provides you and your guests with new plants for the garden. What could be better?

All you need for a simple, elegant arrangement is a small decorative window box or a similar planter and several six-packs and thumb-size, 2-inch pots of blooming bedding plants from the garden center or grocery. Drop the six-packs into the window box, set individual plants around the table as place-card holders or party favors, and you're done!

Once you've enjoyed the temporary planting and the party draws to a close, give your guests their place-card holder plants as a remembrance of the evening. Plan to add your bedding plants to the garden within the next few days. There they can spread out their roots and bloom until season's end, all the while serving as reminders of a pleasant evening spent with your friends.

Materials and Equipment

- One 18-inch-long decorative window box or any similar planter for each table
- Permanent marker

The Plants
shown on the opposite page

- Three six-packs of bedding plants for the planter
- Additional six-packs or thumb-pot plants for place-card holders

Plan of Action

1 Have on hand a window box or planter that suits your dining area.
2 When shopping for your party, pick up at least three six-packs of bedding plants for the centerpiece and additional six-packs or a 2-inch plant for each guest. Choose flowers that will look appropriate on the dining table and, later, in the garden.
3 Plop the six-packs in the planters.
4 When you set the table, place a plant at each place setting. Using a permanent marker, write the guest's name on the pot or on the plant tag.
5 Give the plants new homes after the party—in your guests' gardens and yours.

Packs of flowering annuals such as wax begonias slip inside a decorative wood planter for a dining-table centerpiece. Later, they can be transplanted to larger pots or the garden.

Bedding All-Stars for Summer-Long Color

A ANNUAL SAGE (*Salvia splendens, Salvia coccinea,* and *Salvia farinacea*) comes in both hot and cool colors. The plants love sun and heat; moist, well-drained soil; and light feedings of all-purpose, water-soluble plant food.

B MARIGOLDS are among the easiest, most rewarding annual flowers for beginners of all ages. The dwarf, or French, types (*Tagetes patula*) spread into low, flower-covered mounds. Give the plants sun, and snap off the dead flowers.

C WAX BEGONIA is a classic bedding annual with waxy green or reddish-brown leaves and single or double flowers that may be white, pink, rose, or brick red. Plants like sun to half shade and moist soil.

D CUPFLOWER is a graceful, mounding or trailing annual with small leaves and quarter-size white or blue-purple flowers. Give it sun to half shade, moist soil, and light feedings of all-purpose water-soluble plant food.

E NEMESIA is an annual that grows clouds of small, sweetly scented flowers on upright to cascading plants about 15 inches tall and wide. Newer colors include mauve, pink, and blue. Sun to half shade and moist soil.

BEDDING PLANTS, those annual all-stars, are born to shine for one season only. The plants stand up and spread colors under the hottest sun. The blooms keep coming until frost, or seeds are set. Then the plants have finished their cycle, and you can add them to the compost pile. In warmest climates and southern coastal gardens, annuals can be planted in fall for blooms in winter and earliest spring, until the tropical heat does them in.

Every new gardening season brings a crop of new varieties. Plant breeders constantly strive to produce plants of outstanding vigor and nonstop blooms in fun new colors that combine easily.

Bedding plants acquired the name from Victorian gardeners, who filled tidy beds with colorful annuals in patterned rows. If your goal is to have masses of bloom in a hurry, use the minimum spacing requirements noted on the variety label of the plants you buy at the garden center.

Salvia splendens 'Hot Shot' and *Salvia farinacea* 'Rhea'

Tagetes patula

Begonia semperflorens-cultorem

Nierembergia 'Purple Robe'

Nemesia strumosa

Planting Bedding Plants

USE THIS TECHNIQUE to get plants off to a good start and keep them going with a little maintenance and a lot of productivity.

1 In a new or established bed, the better the soil, the more successful the plantings. Mix in soil amendments, such as packaged garden soil, compost, or composted manure.

2 Spread a 2-inch layer of mulch over the planting area.

3 Arrange plants on top of mulch using the recommended minimum or maximum spacing shown below.

4 As you plant, pull back mulch enough to dig a planting hole. Use a trowel (in well-cultivated soil your hand may do) to make holes slightly larger than the plant's root ball. Place the plant in the planting hole at the same level it was in the pack cell. Refill the hole, pressing soil around the root ball. Keep mulch a hand's width away from the plant. Feed regularly with all-purpose plant food throughout the season.

Bedding plants are sold in packs of three, four, six, or eight cells. Usually six or eight packs make a flat. Space plants so beds are full but not crowded. Spacing (as indicated on the plant tag) depends on the variety, the mature size of plants, and rate of growth. For a uniform look, use measured spacing, positioning plants in rows with equal space between plants. Space closer together for faster effect and farther apart for economy.

When preparing soil, dig only enough to roughly mix in amendments. Pinch the bottom of the pack to release the plant. Gently poke a fingertip into the bottom of the root ball and wiggle it to loosen

the roots. Water each plant well at the outset and be prepared to water more until roots are established. Use

▲ Maximum spacing requirements listed on the variety label allow you to use fewer plants. This spacing is better suited to a long growing season than a short one.

a transplant starting solution at planting, then continue to feed regularly with all–purpose plant food.

▲ Minimum spacing requirements for fast coverage are also listed on the variety label. Planting too close may result in stunted, disappointing growth.

Big pots filled with the same mixture of plants create a unity that spells big impact for less work. Big pots don't dry out as quickly as smaller ones. They are more stable in windy settings, and the soil stays cooler in hottest weather.

Think Big When Staging a Party

Transform a spacious but dull deck into pure theater with huge containers for dramatic effect. Then put that deck to good use—and invite your friends over for a party.

That deck out back that's functional but plain could become a party room. Take a cue from set designers and create an attractive space for entertaining or gathering with the family by thinking BIG.

Everyone will want to hang out on your deck when it looks as beautiful and inviting as the one shown. The trick to setting the scene is simple: Plant six huge pots of spectacular color. These planting schemes harness the power of multiples; repeating them adds impact. Three background planters feature a simple single-color purple scheme that's designed for height and dramatic impact. Three accent planters include a broader color palette in yellow, chartreuse, purple, and silvery whites with a variety of fast-growing and showy plants. The planters stage a nonstop show from late spring through autumn.

Whether you're planning to build a new deck or update an old one, include extra seating as part of the deck's design. Stairs, built-in benches along rails, and planter walls all provide places to sit. A large outdoor umbrella creates shelter and shade from the hot afternoon sun. You can string twinkle lights under the umbrella for night festivities and position votives or luminarias both for their sparkling effect and to guide guests in the dark.

Materials and Equipment
(to make six planters)

- Six 24" to 30" polystyrene pots
- Six 2-cubic-foot bags of premium potting mix

The Plants
shown on the opposite page

- For each sun-loving background planter: One 6" purple fountain grass (*Pennisetum*); four 4" purple fan flower (*Scaevola*)
- For each sun-loving accent planter: One 6" yellow strawflower and one each 3" 'Marguerite' sweet potato vine, multiflora petunia, licorice plant, and purple fan flower

Plan of Action

1 Make three background planters and three accent planters suited to the location (sun or shade). Gather the materials in spring as soon as danger of frost is past. Set planters in place on the deck, and preferably on casters, prior to planting.

2 Drill a ½- to 1-inch drainage hole in the bottom of each planter if none exists.

3 Fill the container two-thirds full of potting mix.

4 Remove the plants from their nursery pots and set in place on top of the potting mix. Add more mix, filling between the plants and covering the root balls.

5 Water well with a water-soluble starting plant food. Through the growing season, water as needed to keep the soil moist but not soggy—avoid overwatering. Feed regularly with all-purpose plant food.

▲ Gaining Privacy with Beauty
Three large background planters add color and drama to the outdoor living area. Set on a bench for added height, they screen the neighbor's view and provide enclosure.

▲ A Simple Color Scheme
Each background planter requires only five plants that fill out quickly. The single-color scheme simplifies plant selection and exemplifies the idea that less is more.

▲ Place the Accent Here
Accent planters call attention to themselves and also can serve to indicate an entrance or the beginning of steps.

Ideal Container Partners

A PURPLE FOUNTAIN GRASS is grown as an annual in cold climates. Give it full sun. Once established in beds or containers, it is drought-resistant. It enhances almost all flower and leaf colors. It is perennial in Zones 7–11, where it spreads aggressively by seed.

B STRAWFLOWERS are annuals that are unfazed by sun and heat. They dry on their own when cut and look fresh almost indefinitely. Give them a half day or more of full sun. Water to establish; once established, the plants tolerate dryness.

C LEMON VERBENA is a shrubby herb that you can winter over in any frost-free place. Give it sun and companion flowering plants. The leaves smell of lemon; use them to garnish cold drinks.

D 'DRAGON WINGS' BEGONIA has arching stems with waxy, angel-wing leaves and scarlet or soft pink flowers in astonishing numbers. Provide sun to half shade, moist soil, and light feedings of all-purpose water-soluble plant food.

E NEW GUINEA IMPATIENS needs more direct sun than ordinary varieties. This annual thrives in moist soil and with regular feedings of all-purpose water-soluble plant food. Deadheading the large spent flowers helps plant health.

ike guests at a dinner party, some plants have instant rapport. They play off one another's best qualities and enhance the overall gathering. Keeping an eye on the general effect, you soon recognize the ideal companions: tall and short, cascading and bushy, flowers and foliage. You also know better than to mix colors that clash or shade-lovers with sun worshipers. Companionable plants combine on the basis of colors, textures, forms, sizes, and rates of growth. An upright herb complements a bushier bloomer, for instance. A roundy-moundy plant completes any composition at the edge, especially if the plant has white, pink, blue, or yellow flowers that blend easily with other colors. Not all plants are perfect in every way, but they are favored for one reason or another. These plants often benefit from the presence of other plants, as one's strengths balance the other's weak spots. Together, their colors pop and their forms fit in harmony.

A

Pennisetum setaceum

B

Helichrysum bracteatum 'Bright Bikinis'

C

Aloysia tryphylla

D

Begonia 'Dragon Wings'

E

Impatiens hawkeri 'Celebretta Purple'

Planting in Big Containers

1

2

3

4

MORE IS BETTER Why wait months for flowers? Get the biggest effect possible in the least amount of time by planting large containers with as many plants as you can fit in. You'll need at least 15 plants in 3- or 4-inch nursery pots to fill the 18-inch container shown.

1 Fill the pot with a premium potting mix to within 6 inches of its rim. Work with plants in 3- or 4-inch pots. Set the still-potted plants in the container and move them around until you like the composition. Place the tallest plants in the center and the shortest ones around the perimeter.

2 Begin slipping the plants out of their nursery pots and placing them in the planter shoulder to shoulder.

3 .Fill around the plants with enough potting mix to fill the planter. Use chopsticks to push the potting mix into every nook and cranny. When you are finished planting, water in well to settle the potting mix. Fill in with more mix if necessary, and water again.

4 Water and feed the plants regularly and generously to compensate for their crowded roots. They will grow and produce a mature look within four to six weeks.

CHANGE PLANT PARTNERS with the seasons. When spring turns to summer, replace a cool-season bloomer with a heat-tolerant one.

1 'Penola', a pansy-viola hybrid, thrives through the cool weeks of spring in a mostly shaded pot.

2 'Elfin' impatiens also prefers shade and takes over in summer where the penolas leave off.

1

2

"DON'T BE AFRAID to crowd those plants in pots! They adapt to the container and slow down their growth."

—Peter Strauss

In this chapter

134 SMALL-SPACE VEGETABLE BEDS
Make attractive raised vegetable beds in minutes.

136 Plants: Small-Space Vegetables
137 Technique: Starting Plants from Seed Indoors

138 A PRIVACY SCREEN
THAT PRODUCES
Enjoy privacy while you harvest loads of tomatoes
in front of a south-facing porch.

140 Plants: Vegetables That Climb
141 Technique: Improving Soil

142 PORTABLE CUT-FLOWER GARDEN
Grow a portable cutting garden with zinnias in pots.

144 Plants: Cut Flowers for Containers
145 Technique: Staking Flowers

146 GROW YOUR OWN ORANGES,
LEMONS, AND LIMES
Grow dwarf citrus in pots and reap an exotic harvest.

148 Plants: Best Dwarf Citrus
149 Technique: Repotting a Container Plant

150 HANGING HERBS
Keep a selection of fresh kitchen herbs in easy reach:
Grow them in a three-tiered, moss-lined hanging basket.

152 Plants: Kitchen Herbs for Hanging Baskets
153 Technique: Planting Hanging Baskets
with Coir Liner

154 LETTUCE FOR
BEAUTY AND BOUNTY
Sow attractive varieties of lettuce between bulbs
and let them take over when the blooms are done.

156 Plants: Lettuce for Every Season
157 Technique: Direct-Sowing Seeds

Gardens That Produce

Vegetable and cut-flower gardens bigger than a city lot and commercial truck gardens measured in acres are supplying farmer's markets everywhere with freshness and variety that ignite tastebuds and fill vases with blooms. On a much smaller scale, you can grow salad items, vegetables, savory herbs, fruits, and cut flowers in ways that make the productive garden a showplace in its own right. Where space is limited, go vertical. Container plantings let you grow tomatoes on the terrace and herbs only steps away from the kitchen or the grill. Pots of lettuce make beautiful foliage. Enjoy!

Small-Space Vegetable Beds

Some might call it a *potager* (French for kitchen garden), but you will call it the perfect way to grow a harvest of fresh produce in a limited space.

▲ Lay Out Beds
Use twine and stakes, then apply spray marker.

▲ Remove Sod
Use shovel to cut along spray lines.

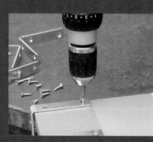

▲ Cultivate Soil
Turn soil to approximate depth of spade, then smooth until level.

▲ Build Frames
Secure corners with L braces. At corners drive stakes and fasten to frame with screws.

▲ Fill Raised Bed
Use packaged garden soil.

Designed as a grid of raised beds and surrounding paths, this garden is intended to be both decorative and practical. It employs an intensive approach, popularized by French gardeners, that combines vegetables, herbs, flowers, and fruits in small, highly productive beds, and it provides a pleasing view from the house. Small beds make it possible to plant, tend, and harvest from the paths.

The garden shown was made by framing four raised beds with 1×8 cedar planks. Painted bright colors, fastened with L braces and secured to the ground with 18-inch stakes, and filled with premium garden soil, the 30-inch-square beds are ready to grow.

You can cultivate ongoing crops from season to season if your climate permits. For example, early spring lettuce and peas give way to mesclun and herbs that fill in quickly. Summer green beans, carrots, and beets move out in time for fall or winter crops of broccoli and Brussels sprouts.

To keep the garden looking tidy while seasonal crops come and go, edge the beds with compact low growers such as viola, bush basil, or Italian parsley. To use vertical space (and add another dimension), stand a tepee in some beds for climbing vegetables such as cucumbers, or vines such as scarlet runner bean.

Materials and Equipment

- For each raised bed: four 1×8 cedar boards 30" long; eight L braces with deck screws
- For securing in place each raised bed: four 1×2 wood stakes 18" long; deck screws
- One 2-cubic-foot bag of packaged garden soil for each bed
- Pavers (optional); exterior latex paint

The Plants
shown on the opposite page

- Start with packets of seeds or set out transplants. Over time you will find it expedient to set out transplants when you see them for sale at your nursery. Or sow seeds of something that grows quickly, such as lettuce, which is ready to pick in about 45 days.

Plan of Action

1 Site the garden within convenient reach of the kitchen. A sunny location protected from north winds is best. A nearby source of water is essential.

2 Lay out beds within the available space in a patterned design. Leave space between beds wide enough to accommodate a wheelbarrow or a mower.

3 Build raised-bed frames using weather-resistant lumber painted a bright color as shown, concrete blocks, or stacked stone. Make paths of pavers or turf.

4 Fill beds with packaged garden soil; top-dress with compost in fall or winter.

5 Interplant quick crops (leaf lettuce) with slower-maturing crops (cabbage). As soon as one crop finishes, plant another. Dense planting thwarts weeds. To maximize harvests feed regularly throughout the season with all-purpose or vegetable-specific plant food.

Here's an attractive, productive little kitchen garden you can build, plant, and have the satisfaction of finishing in one morning. Bright paint color makes for cheerful beds even in a wintry landscape, with or without snow.

BEFORE

Small-Space Vegetables

A TOMATO varieties that form bushes (determinate) instead of vines are suited to limited spaces. Names to watch for: 'Bushel Basket', 'Super Bush', 'Tiny Tim', 'Patio Prize', 'Small Fry', and 'Toy Boy'.

B PEPPERS can be sweet, hot, or specially bred for pickling or drying. Watch for compact varieties: 'Ace', 'Jingle Bells', 'Cherrytime', 'Sweet Banana', 'Lipstick', and 'Super Cayenne II'.

C CARROTS The ball- or finger-shape varieties are best in limited space. Sow seeds sparsely where they are to grow. Try 'Baby Finger', 'Short 'n Sweet', 'Thumbelina', and 'Kundulus'.

D BUSH BEANS can be green, yellow, lima, or shell (navy, northern, red kidney, black turtle). The bushes reach 15 to 24 inches tall and wide, and they add attractive, leafy greenery to the garden.

E PEARL ONION is a small bulb formed while the plant is young. Plant a short-day onion variety ('1015Y Texas Supersweet', 'Yellow Granex', 'White Bermuda') in a long-day (15 hours) climate.

THE VEGETABLES BEST SUITED FOR SMALL-SPACE gardens are compact with confined growth habits but full-size produce. The list includes salad greens, beet, radish, carrot, pepper, onion, eggplant, chard, choy, bush tomato (determinate), and bush varieties of bean, pea, squash, and cucumber.

Alternatively, you can grow dwarf or patio varieties. Descriptions on seed packages or plant labels indicate space-saving plants good for containers.

Grow the vegetables that you use and enjoy the most. Choose vegetables with ornamental appeal and be innovative in the way you plant them. Frame beds with an edge of tidy hot peppers or alternating red and white radishes. If you prefer cherry or pear tomatoes, which are vining (indeterminate), you'll need to station a sturdy trellis against a wall or on one side of the garden.

Tomato 'Minibel'

Sweet bell pepper 'Lipstick'

Carrot 'Thumbelina'

Bush bean 'Maxibel Filet'

Onion 'Crystal Wax'

Starting Plants from Seed Indoors

▲ Moisten the seed-starting mix, then fill the cell-pack containers to just below their brims with the moistened mix.

▲ Wet the tip of a lead pencil and use it to pick up individual seeds and plant them in the center of a cell.

▲ Place seed trays in a warm spot, such as the top of the refrigerator. If seeds need dark to germinate, cover the trays.

▲ After seeds have been planted in each cell of the flat, sift some seed-starter mix over the cell-pack to cover seeds.

▲ Keep soil moist until germination. If the surface dries slightly, use a clean mister filled with warm water to moisten it.

▲ Move seedlings to a brightly lit spot. They need fresh air circulation (but not drafts) to develop into sturdy plants.

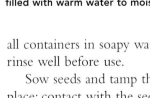

▲ A fluorescent-light setup is ideal for starting seeds. Keep leaves about 4 inches from the tubes.

Sowing seeds indoors gives plants a head start. To figure out when to start seeds indoors, refer to the seed packet for the germination time, how long to transplant, and the best time to plant outdoors.

Use a special seed-starting mix and plastic containers. Whether you buy or reuse flats of cell packs, you'll need watertight trays to set under them and lids or sheet plastic to cover them. If you like, recycle the cell-pack containers you get from garden centers. Wash all containers in soapy water and rinse well before use.

Sow seeds and tamp them in place; contact with the seed-starting mix promotes germination. Make sure very small seeds and those that require light to germinate lie directly on the surface. Seeds have varying requirements to germinate: either warmth or cold; light or darkness—consult the seed packet before planting. Keep the cell packs moist until germination. Water seedlings from the bottom by pouring water into the tray.

"START SEEDS to encourage children's interest in gardening. Start pumpkins, marigolds, and sunflowers. Watch the amazement!"

—Peter Strauss

Training tomatoes takes only a little time each week, and the result is a tidy plant that bears heavily. The heirloom 'Black Plum' (above) has a savory, almost salty taste. The bed pictured (right) features green and purple basil and sweet and hot peppers in front of the tomatoes.

Heirloom tomatoes ▶ come in many sizes, shapes, and colors. Each has a distinctive taste.

A Privacy Screen That Produces

Grow heirloom or hybrid tomatoes up a twine trellis on the sunny side of a porch and you'll get a fast-growing privacy screen that's both decorative and fruitful.

▲ Start with a Ground Stake
Drive the stake into the ground to anchor. Tie jute roping through a hole in stake.

Growing tomatoes within arm's reach of the kitchen means more than immediate gratification. This project provides privacy as well as shade, saves gardening space, and promises a high yield of tomatoes.

For centuries, gardeners have used woody plants, such as certain apples or pears, as subjects for espalier (es-PAL-yay), in which branches are trained horizontally on wires to develop a two-dimensional form that has height and width but not much depth. This project simplifies espalier by training vining tomatoes up cordons of jute rope.

Growing tomatoes up a rope trellis yields advantages: You'll avoid the hassle of conventional staking or caging when the tomatoes typically outgrow their supports and become less productive. And you can easily see and reach fruits on the neat, upright vines.

You can adapt this garden on the porch to suit a deck, a gazebo, or an arbor. As long as you grow indeterminate tomatoes, which are vining by nature, your choice of varieties is vast. Plan to grow a beefsteak variety for slicing; a plum type for sauce; and a cherry, pear, or grape tomato for snacks and salads.

▲ Attach Ropes Above
Directly above the ground stake, install a screw eye in the eave. Tie the rope taut.

Materials and Equipment

- One spool of jute rope
- Ten 1×2 wood stakes 1' long
- Cordless drill
- Scissors or utility knife
- Eight screw eyes
- One roll of hook-and-loop fasteners

The Plants
shown on the opposite page

- Eight indeterminate tomato plants
- Two 4" compact basil plants
- Two 4" purple-leaf basil plants
- One 4" hot pepper plant
- Two 4" sweet pepper plants
- Four 2-cubic-foot bags of garden soil for flowers and vegetables

▲ Pinch Out the Suckers
Remove side branches as soon as they diverge from the main leader.

Plan of Action

1 On south- or west-facing site, prepare planting bed with premium garden soil. Tomatoes are heavy feeders; add slow-release plant food before planting.

2 Drill a ½-inch hole in the top end of each wood stake. Then set them 16 inches apart down the length of the bed. In the eave directly above each stake, install a screw eye. Tie a length of jute rope taut between each stake and the screw eye that corresponds to it.

3 Set an indeterminate tomato next to each stake. In front of the row of tomatoes, set the green and purple basil plants and the sweet and hot peppers.

4 As each tomato grows, tie the main stem (leader) loosely to the rope; repeat after each 12 inches or so of new growth. Remove any suckers (side branches different from the main leader) as soon as you detect them.

5 Water to keep soil moist. Avoid watering foliage to reduce potential for disease. Feed with water-soluble tomato plant food every two weeks. Harvest in 70 to 90 days. The more you pick, the more the vines will yield.

▲ Tie Tomato Vines to Rope
Use hook-and-loop fasteners (or plant ties) to hold the tomato vine to the rope.

Vegetables That Climb

A TOMATO Indeterminate (vining) varieties continue to grow and produce all season. Choose from many colors, fruit sizes, and flavors. Pinch out side shoots (suckers) as soon as you see them diverge from the main stalk.

B POLE BEAN seeds are sown in the garden as soon as the soil is warm. Plant seeds around an 8-foot tepee or at the bottom of a twine grid stretched between strong uprights. Harvest frequently.

C CUCUMBER vines climb via coiling tendrils on a wire fence or twine netting. When plants reach 4 to 5 feet, pinch out the main growing tip to encourage side shoots, more flowers, and more fruit.

D PEA varieties include snow (edible pod), snap, or shelling types. Plant seeds in earliest spring; peas thrive in cool weather. Provide the support of a wire or twine net, or 3- to 4-foot branch trimmings ("brush").

E MALABAR SPINACH, or Indian spinach, is a vining hot-weather substitute for true spinach (which prefers cool weather). Grow it in sun, planted around a 6- to 8-foot tepee. The stems are purple and the leaves are eaten like regular spinach.

IN MOST CASES, VINING, TWINING, AND SCRAMBLING plants need plenty of room to grow. If you take advantage of vertical space, your garden can reach new heights—even in a small space.

Give climbing vegetables the support they need to reach for the sky via a decorative trellis or a fence. Other types of supports include mesh netting or twine stretched between posts; tepees of bamboo, rebar, or other tall stakes; and arched bentwood tunnels. For tomatoes, many gardeners swear by cylindrical towers of steel-wire fencing anchored with substantial stakes. Depending on your garden's exposure, place climbing vegetables at the back, sides, or center of the site where they won't shade other plants. Set supports in place at planting time to avoid disturbing roots. As plants grow, guide them up the support and secure them with loose, flexible ties. Supports need to be as tall as the plant grows and strong enough to hold against wind.

Tomato 'Big Beef'

Pole bean 'Blue Lake'

Cucumber 'Marketmore'

Pea 'Super Sugar Snap Improved'

Malabar spinach

Improving Soil

▲ Tilling is most readily accomplished when the soil is moist, neither dry nor wet. Go over the area once, then add soil amendments. Till in two directions in order to mix the amendments well with the native soil. Rake afterward to smooth out and level the bed.

ASSESSING SOIL TEXTURE

▲ When squeezed, a handful of heavy, poorly draining clay soil forms a sticky, hard mass. Improve it with loads of organic matter (not sand, which turns the muck into concrete).

▲ A handful of sandy soil only crumbles. It holds neither water nor nutrients. As with clay soil, the answer to improving sandy soil is to work in lots of organic matter.

▲ Good loam holds its shape when squeezed; it also crumbles when poked with a finger.

How would you characterize your soil? In order to improve it, you must first identify your soil type. Is it the red clay of the Southeast, the sandy clay of Texas, or the caliche (sandy, rocky, alkaline stuff) of Arizona? Is it boggy muck that drains poorly and lacks nutrients? Or are you fortunate to have good loam, a rich balance of humus, sand, and clay? Ideal garden soil is easy to work; it holds enough air, water, and nutrients to sustain plant growth.

Soil provides the key to your garden's success. The type and quality of your garden's soil affects the plants' vitality as well as how you'll spend time working to improve it. Even gardens with good soil benefit from regular additions of organic amendments, added to improve the soil's fertility along with its ability to hold and drain moisture. If you improve the soil, you increase the plants' chances of surviving and thriving. Stress from poor soil makes plants vulnerable to predatory insects and diseases.

Organic amendments include compost, chopped leaves, grass clippings, and rotted manure. Apply each season and whenever you plant. Organic matter attracts earthworms to the garden. The more earthworms in your garden, the healthier your soil will be.

> "NOTHING TAKES THE PLACE OF GOOD SOIL.
> Ideally, preparation should be done before anything has been planted. If you can manage to prepare soil in fall, so much the better. Winter works its magic by the time spring rolls around."
>
> —Peter Strauss

Portable Cut-Flower Garden

▲ Sow Zinnia Seeds in a Big Pot
Fill a 15-inch pot with potting mix and scatter zinnia seeds over the surface. Lightly cover them with more mix. Keep warm and moist.

▲ Thin Out the Weaker Seedlings When the zinnia seedlings have one or two sets of true leaves, snip off all but the strongest seedlings. Leave about eight equally spaced seedlings in the pot.

▲ Thinned Seedlings Grow Fat
One of the joys of container gardens is that you can move them around as needed. These are the same zinnias shown in the photo on the opposite page.

Grow pots of zinnias from seed and nurture them in a sunny place. When they bloom, move the pots anywhere you like, or make bouquets for the house.

Keep a supply of flowering plants on hand for cutting fresh bouquets all summer and fall. Planting them in lightweight pots results in movable eye candy. When fully blooming the pots are easily moved to jazz up an entry or outdoor living area.

Zinnias are old-fashioned favorites that thrive in sunny, hot weather. Their vivid blooms make outstanding cut flowers that last up to two weeks. Choose from a variety of zinnias for different effects in the garden (select the taller varieties for cut flowers). The flowers range from diminutive, star-shape blooms to giant, 6-inch dahlia look-alikes. No matter which variety you grow, you'll appreciate their cut-and-come-again nature: The more you snip, the more they'll bloom.

Zinnias are easy to grow from seed. Plant seeds directly into pots of moist, fresh potting mix. Add about ¼ inch of potting mix on top of the seeds. After the seedlings show one or two sets of true leaves, thin them to stand 3 or 4 inches apart.

Zinnias need full sun and a place where air circulates freely. Water well when the surface soil feels dry, ideally before the leaves wilt. Feed with all-purpose water-soluble plant food according to label directions. After frost, remove the dead plants and save the pots for another season.

Materials and Equipment

- Six 15" terra-cotta color plastic pots
- Three 2-cubic-foot bags of premium potting mix
- All-purpose plant food

The Plants
shown on the opposite page

- Three packets of zinnia seeds in mix or match colors and types: 'Lilliput', cactus-flowered, 'Candy Cane' (striped), giants, or 'Cut and Come Again'

Plan of Action

1 Fill pots with potting mix to about an inch from the top. Tamp down lightly.
2 Scatter zinnia seeds over the soil surface. Cover with about ¼ inch of potting mix. Again, tamp down lightly. Water well.
3 Set the seeded pots in a sunny, warm place. Keep the soil evenly moist.
4 When the seedlings have been growing a few weeks, you will see they each have one or two sets of true leaves above the original sprout leaves. Thin from each group using scissors or pruners, leaving the strongest seedlings, about eight in each pot, spaced 3 or 4 inches apart.
5 Feed with all-purpose plant food according to label directions. Cut lots of bouquets and enjoy!

◀ Zinnias are the quintessential bouquet flowers of summer. When you grow them in pots, they also come in handy for bringing cheerful color to entry steps and to any outdoor living area such as a porch.

805

Cut Flowers for Containers

A ZINNIAS are annuals that come in many flower sizes, shapes, and colors, and plant heights. Choose from golf-ball to saucer size flowers in cool to hot colors. Provide full sun and water well before the leaves wilt.

B MARIGOLD varieties may be dwarf or tall, but for cutting you want the tallest African varieties available. All marigolds are annuals with yellow, orange, or nearly white flowers. They bloom freely until the first killing frost in fall.

C AGERATUM is an annual best known for squat plant mounds and fuzzy blue flowers. Now, however, varieties are being developed especially for the cutting garden. Watch for transplants at your garden center.

D DIANTHUS is the botanical name for carnation, sweet William, and pinks. Newly developed annual varieties have long, wiry stems and are wonderful for adding color and clove scent to flower arrangements.

E SNAPDRAGON varieties, such as the Rocket series, grow to 36 inches tall and make long-lasting cut flowers. In Zones 9 and 10, set out transplants in early fall for blooms in winter and spring.

CONTAINER GARDENS ENTAIL MINIMAL work once they're planted. For sources of generous bouquets, rely on the tried-and-true flowering annuals that have delighted generations of gardeners. In addition to the flowers listed, consider planting calendula, plume celosia, larkspur, flowering tobacco, blue salvia, and stock in containers. Grow tall varieties with long stems for the best results. Most of the annuals noted do best in full sun with ample drainage. Cut them frequently to keep the plants bushy, compact, and producing more buds. Plant seeds in pots of moist soil or set out transplants from the garden center. In regions that have a short growing season, annuals that take months to bloom need to be started indoors. Sow seed six to eight weeks before the plants are to be set outdoors (after frost danger). Check the soil daily during hot weather and water potted plants thoroughly (until water runs out the bottom of the pot). Feed weekly with all-purpose water-soluble plant food for vigorous plants and larger blooms.

A *Zinnia elegans 'Bouquet'*

B *Tagetes erecta*

C *Ageratum 'Blue Horizon'*

D *Dianthus 'Amazon Neon Cherry'*

E *Antirrhinum majus 'Rocket Hybrid'*

Staking Flowers

▲ Slender stakes, intended to hide among tall plant stems, pose an eye-poking risk. Sheath them decoratively.

▲ Tie tall plant stems to stakes using a figure-eight technique, which allows the plant room to grow without becoming strangled by the plant tie.

▲ Round, grow-through supports of an open grid design work well for peonies and bellflowers.

Twiggy, ▶ branched trimmings from trees or shrubs make natural stakes for tall Asiatic lilies and other plants that need a bit of support.

▲ Tomato cages work well as supports for plants with heavy, substantial flowers, such as dahlias.

Stake tall or floppy plants to keep them upright and prevent damage if the plant falls or blows over. Many of the best plant supports do their jobs unobtrusively. Position a stake, a grow-through ring, or other support early in the season. It will vanish among the stems and leaves as the plant grows.

Lend support to the plants that need it most: tall, slender gladiolus, delphiniums, foxgloves, and lilies; bushy plants that tend to flop over, such as Shasta daisies, asters, yarrow, and false indigo *(Baptisia)*. For large-flowered dahlias, set a stake at the time the tuber is planted; wire cages sold for tomatoes can substitute for the conventional staking.

Choose sturdy supports designed to blend with the surroundings and endure weather without rotting or rusting, such as bamboo stakes or hoops and stakes made of powder-coated, heavy-gauge green wire. If you live in a cold area, remove supports from the garden in fall and store them over winter to extend their life and utility.

"STAKING WORKS BEST if you train the plant before rather than after it has grown big and a storm has blown it over. Install stakes early so that growing plants camouflage them and they don't become eyesores."

—Peter Strauss

Potted citrus trees bring a tropical touch to a sunny room, especially in winter. If you start with a three- or four-year-old tree, you'll soon enjoy its fruit. Citrus plants need bright sunlight and added humidity to fare best indoors.

Grow Your Own Oranges, Lemons, and Limes

No matter where you live, you can grow dwarf citrus in pots and enjoy the glossy, waxy leaves; the fragrant flowers in season; and the ripening, colorful fruits.

Citrus plants seem to have it all: evergreen, glossy foliage; a season of ornamental and delicious fruit; and flowers that fill rooms with their coveted fragrance. The dwarf trees and shrubs flourish in warm-climate landscapes and can be grown anywhere indoors. In cold-winter climates, potted citrus plants do best in a cool greenhouse, a sunroom, or a basement under grow-lights.

You can choose from many varieties of citrus, from lemon, lime, orange, and grapefruit to kumquat, tangerine, calamondin orange, and others. Although it's possible to grow most citrus from seeds salvaged from store-bought fruit, you'll find dwarf varieties that are vastly superior for container growing.

Citrus plants grown indoors need direct sunlight in order to produce flowers and fruit. Any sunny window, other than a northern exposure, is fine. Temperatures between 60 and 80°F and moderate humidity are ideal. Set your potted plant on a waterproof tray filled with pebbles and water to boost humidity. Water regularly to keep soil moist. Set citrus plants outside to summer on the deck or patio or in the garden.

You can keep true dwarf citrus vital and vigorous in 15- to 18-inch pots for many years. Shower dusty leaves clean and be sure to feed faithfully in spring and summer.

Materials and Equipment
- 18" terra-cotta pot
- Packaged premium potting mix. Make sure the potting mix contains composted bark fines (finely ground bark) and sphagnum peat moss.

The Plants
shown on the opposite page
- Dwarf lemon, lime, or orange tree

Plan of Action
1 Pot a three- to four-year-old plant in an 18-inch-diameter container.
2 Feed year-round, using a dilute solution of plant food such as 30-10-10. During hot weather, potted citrus outdoors will likely need daily watering.
3 Protect citrus plants from temperatures below freezing. Move them indoors over winter before frost threatens in fall.
4 If brown scale, mealybugs, aphids, or spider mites attack, spray at weekly intervals with insecticidal soap until the infestation clears completely.

▲ **Warmth + Sun = Fruit**
Place potted citrus trees outdoors in a warm microclimate: next to a concrete sidewalk or driveway, on the south side of the house, or on the sunny side of a wall.

▲ **Lemons All Winter**
Lemon trees are among the most rewarding of indoor/outdoor plants. They get high marks for glossy leaves, fragrant flowers, and colorful, edible fruit.

▲ **You Be the Bee**
To aid pollination and ensure fruiting, use a fine paintbrush to transfer pollen grains from the stamens of a flower to the pistils in the center of other flowers.

Best Dwarf Citrus

A MEYER LEMON is one of the most popular citrus for pots. The large, round, slightly orange fruits have a thin skin and a tangy flavor that's favored by chefs for any dish calling for a lemony taste.

B MEXICAN (KEY) LIME varieties produce small, aromatic, round green-to-yellow fruits on trees that reach 12 feet when grown in the garden. Authentic for Key lime pie and superb for afternoon tea.

C CLEMENTINE TANGERINE is a mandarin orange variety that grows into a small tree with an attractive weeping form and dense foliage. In warm climates it can produce a lot of fruit if pollinators, such as 'Dancy' or 'Kinnow' mandarins, are nearby.

D KUMQUAT forms a dense, 4-foot-tall shrub that's hardier than most citrus. The fruit has an edible, spicy-sweet rind and tart, juicy flesh. The plants are often trained as bonsai specimens.

E CALAMONDIN is called dwarf orange, although it is actually a sour-acid mandarin or kalamonsi. The inch-round orange fruits are best cooked into marmalade; they are too tart for eating out of hand.

Most citrus plants grow well in containers, although some are especially well-suited to pot culture (see list at left). Dwarf varieties make excellent candidates for containers and reach 4 to 6 feet tall indoors, larger if they live outdoors or at least spend summers there. Whether grown indoors or outdoors, in pots or in the ground, dwarf citrus need the following for the greatest rewards: eight to 12 hours of sunlight daily; temperatures between 60 and 85°F; well-drained soil enriched with pine bark, sphagnum peat moss, and plant food; infrequent but consistent watering to keep soil damp (neither soggy nor bone dry); and protection from harsh winds. Citrus are especially sensitive to cold and must be sheltered from frost. Lemons are hardier than oranges and grapefruit, but not as hardy as limes. In case of frost threat in a warm climate, hang Christmas tree lights on your in-ground outdoor tree and leave the lights on during chilly nights; also cover the tree with a sheet.

A *Citrus limon* 'Meyer Improved'

B *Citrus aurantiifolia*

C *Citrus reticulata* 'Clementine'

D *Fortunella margarita* 'Nagami'

E × *Citrofortunella microcarpa*

Repotting a Container Plant

1

2

3

4

REPOT CONTAINER PLANTS once a year to promote healthy growth. If a plant often wilts between waterings and needs to be watered more than once a week (besides during hot weather outdoors), repotting is probably in order.

1 You know a plant needs repotting when its dense roots have filled the pot. Carefully scratch away the outer edge of the top of the soil to determine the extent of root development.

2 To repot, gently tip over the plant and slide it out of the pot. For its new home, choose a larger pot with drain hole. Citrus grow best in terra-cotta.

3 Loosen the root ball with your fingertips if the roots have become packed or tightly wound. Shake off any old, loose soil.

4 Fill the bottom of the large pot with fresh potting mix. Set the plant in the pot, filling around the root ball with fresh potting mix. Fill to the same level the plant was potted before. Water until water runs out the pot bottom. Water regularly to keep soil damp to slightly dry at the surface. Feed regularly with plant food formulated for citrus or acid-loving plants.

CONTAINER PLANT GROWTH CYCLE

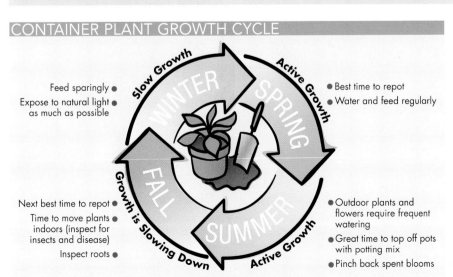

WINTER — Slow Growth
- Feed sparingly
- Expose to natural light as much as possible

SPRING — Active Growth
- Best time to repot
- Water and feed regularly

SUMMER — Active Growth
- Outdoor plants and flowers require frequent watering
- Great time to top off pots with potting mix
- Pinch back spent blooms

FALL — Growth is Slowing Down
- Next best time to repot
- Time to move plants indoors (inspect for insects and disease)
- Inspect roots

"THE BEST TIME TO REPOT OR TRANSPLANT is often the beginning of a season of active growth. Repot container plants at least once a year for best results. I've noticed that successful gardeners are always repotting something."

—Peter Strauss

Hanging Herbs

Hanging baskets have become one of the most popular ways to garden in containers. Filled with herbs, eye-level plantings provide greenery that looks and tastes great.

▲ Starting Solution Jump Start
Soak the long-strand sphagnum moss in a pail of water. Add a starting solution at the outset so it will be absorbed by the moss and ready to boost root growth.

▲ Line with Sphagnum Moss
Wring out the presoaked moss and line each basket, starting with the bottom one. Press into place, then fill the inside cavity with moisture-controlling potting mix.

▲ Plant the Herbs
Remove nursery pots and snuggle the root ball of each plant into the potting mix. Water well, drain, and hang.

Display this ornamental and practical planter near the kitchen, if possible. Enjoy the herbs' bold leaves and savory fragrances outdoors. Bring clippings inside for cooking, or use outside for grilling.

Most herbs grow easily in containers. Wire baskets work well because they promote the proper drainage that herbs require. The plants shown include showy varieties of herbs that need a sunny location: golden marjoram, silver marjoram, and variegated pineapple mint.

The herb world offers you a tantalizing array of plant possibilities. To narrow the choices, aim for culinary herbs. They have both decorative and practical qualities. The marjoram and mint varieties shown, like many herbs, feature smallish leaves and neat, overall patterns of growth. Although most herbs develop flowers, foliage is their strong suit, so look for leaves with pleasing colors or textures.

Let the plants grow for a month before you start harvesting the stem ends. Use marjoram to flavor tomato sauces, soups, and sautéed zucchini. Garnish iced tea or lemonade with sprigs of pineapple mint.

Use a wand attachment on the hose to ease watering. Feed weekly with an all-purpose water-soluble plant food at the dilute rate of 1 teaspoon per gallon of water.

Materials and Equipment

- One three-tier wire mesh hanging basket from a kitchen store
- One bag long-strand sphagnum moss
- Waterproof gloves
- One 1-cubic-foot bag of moisture-controlling potting mix
- Bucket of water

The Plants
shown on the opposite page

- Three 2" pineapple mint
- Three 2" silver marjoram
- One 2" golden marjoram

Plan of Action

1 Round up materials and work in a place where it's OK to make a mess. You'll also need a place to hang the tiered basket while you plant it.
2 Soak the long-strand sphagnum moss in a bucket of water. To prevent potential skin irritation by the moss, wear waterproof gloves while you work with it.
3 Fill one basket at a time, beginning with the bottom one (pineapple mint). Line the basket with sphagnum moss. Add a 3-inch layer of moisture-controlling potting mix, then arrange the plants equidistantly and cover the root balls with potting mix.
4 Continue planting: first the middle basket with silver marjoram, then the smallest basket with golden marjoram.
5 Water well and allow to drain where the drips won't matter. Feed regularly.

Herbs with a graceful, trailing habit and leaves that are attractively variegated make a surprising hanging garden in any sunny spot. The triple-decker effect means more plants and more savory scents in a given growing space.

Kitchen Herbs for Hanging Baskets

A PINEAPPLE MINT has pebbly green leaves with crisp white edging. When brushed, the leaves give off a surprising pineapple scent. Pretty to look at and nice as a garnish for a cold drink.

B ITALIAN PARSLEY has flat leaves and is the favorite parsley for cooking. Start plants from seed about two months before you want to start harvesting, or buy transplants. Parsley needs half sun and water.

C MARJORAM is an oregano relative. One variety has golden-green leaves. It is a well-behaved creeper and trailer that is ideal for edging a hanging basket that receives direct sun.

D SAGE comes in many varieties, varying in leaf size and color, including golden, purple, and 'Tricolor'. Full sun brings out the leaf colors, and pinching out the tips of new growth promotes compact habit.

E THYME used for cooking is usually the tiny-leaved, upright little bush called English or French thyme. Creeping thyme also can be tasty. The number of its varieties is endless; all are wonderful garden plants.

Virtually all of the herbs that are popular in the kitchen can be grown in pots or hanging baskets. The latter is attractive in a kitchen window that receives direct sun from morning through midday or all afternoon. The advantage of a hanging basket in this situation is that you can grow something like parsley on the more shady side and place the sun-lovers next to the window. Or each time you water the basket, turn the hook around so all sides receive equal sunlight. Placement over the kitchen sink also means that you can easily take the basket down and drench the growing medium as well as shower all the leaves clean. When extra water has stopped draining, hang the basket back up. Cared for in this way, your herbs are unlikely to be buggy or dusty, which means they'll grow more luxuriantly and you will feel good about snipping the leaves to use in cooking. You can grow dwarf bush basil in a hanging basket, as well as a small sweet bay, rosemary, and tarragon.

A

Mentha suaveolens 'Variegata'

B

Petroselinum crispum 'Broad Leaf Italian'

C

Origanum onites 'Aureum'

D

Salvia officinalis 'Icterina'

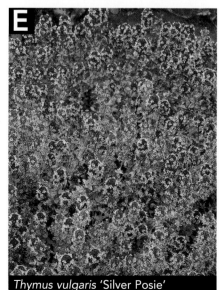

E

Thymus vulgaris 'Silver Posie'

Planting Hanging Baskets
With Coir Liner

1

2

3

4

5

> **"A CLAY POT 12 TO 15 INCHES** in diameter makes a neat place to rest a hanging basket while you're planting. You can also use pots of this size, turned upside down, as stands to show off certain plants in a display."
>
> —Peter Strauss

COIR LINER from coconut husk fiber is long-lasting and organic. It has become the favored material for lining hanging baskets and iron cradles or window boxes.

1 Insert the coir liner into a hanging basket and use pruners or scissors to cut slits in the sides. You will insert root balls of the plants through these slits.

2 Place the basket on top of a big clay pot (it will assist you in holding everything together as you proceed with the planting). After cutting a slit in the coir, open up a pathway with your fingers and gently pull the roots of the plant through until the plant is held firmly against the outside wall. As you work up from the bottom of the basket, add potting mix, working it around the roots of each plant you have inserted through the coir.

3 Once all side plants have been positioned through coir liner and roots are covered, fill basket with more potting mix and add plants to the top.

4 Water the planting thoroughly, so the liner, the soil, and all the roots are completely moistened and no air pockets remain. Drain and hang.

5 Water and feed regularly for lush, vigorous growth.

A big pot with a tree, shrub, or trained vine, such as the Confederate jasmine shown, can provide an ideal place to grow lettuce as a spring or fall crop. Here, the lettuce seeds that were sown when spring bulbs were beginning to bloom are showing mature leaves ready for harvesting.

Lettuce for Beauty and Bounty

Now that lettuce has progressed from ho-hum Iceberg to a food crop that excites the palate, it has also become a thing of beauty that is fun to grow in the garden.

Lettuce has become all at once a plant that gardeners want to grow and chefs covet for making the salad course a treat rather than a treatment that is good for you.

This project demonstrates how you can grow lettuce as both an ornamental and an edible in a space that might otherwise be left bare or filled with flowering plants such as violas and pansies (cool-weather flowers that happen also to be edible). You can use any large container, even those already inhabited by a small tree or shrub, if the branches are high enough above the soil so as not to shade the lettuce too much.

A summer-blooming vine trained on a trellis also may be used as the mainstay for a container garden such as this, with daffodil bulbs planted in fall or, if you live in a frigid climate, added in spring as potted bulbs coming into bloom.

Use a kitchen fork or similar tool to loosen the soil surface around the existing plants, then scatter lettuce seeds over all the bare spaces. Plant thinly to avoid tedious thinning later on. You can mix up two or three kinds of lettuce, or sow different colors in bands or pockets. By the time the bulbs finish blooming and their leaves are starting to mature, the lettuce will be ready to take over and produce a showy, edible crop.

▲ **Sow Lettuce Between Bulbs**
You can sow lettuce seeds in the ground between spring bulbs. The bulb leaves will die down by the time the lettuce leaves are big enough to harvest.

▲ **Thin Lettuce for Fat Results**
Thin lettuce seedlings that come up thickly, so there will be room for the strongest to thrive. As the plants grow, the leaves you cut will be big enough to use in salads.

▲ **Feed Your Lettuce**
Lettuce seedlings grow more vigorously if you feed them at half strength with all-purpose plant food. Doing so also prolongs the harvest.

Materials and Equipment

- One redwood planter tub 24" to 30" in diameter.
- Premium potting mix

The Plants
shown on the opposite page

- One Confederate jasmine trained on a trellis panel
- Twelve daffodil bulbs (or about six potted daffodils coming into bloom)
- Lettuce mix, or two or three different types planted in stripes or broadcast

Plan of Action

1 Find a large tub or pot 24 to 30 inches in diameter, and place it in a sunny, frost-free spot. If you don't already have a tree, a shrub, or a trellised vine for the pot, visit your neighborhood nursery and buy one.

2 In fall, plant the tree, shrub, or vine in the big pot (see page 49 for how to plant a tree or shrub in a container), and plant daffodils around it.

3 You can also start this project at the beginning of the growing season in the spring, and add pots of rooted daffodil bulbs that are growing actively.

4 Sow the lettuce seeds early while temperatures are still cool (35 to 60°F). Scatter over cultivated soil and lightly cover with fresh potting mix.

5 Remove the bulb leaves as they begin to die down. The lettuce will take over and it can be harvested leaf by leaf for a long, productive season.

Lettuce for Every Season

A 'DEER TONGUE' is a loose-leaf green lettuce that does not form a heart and is therefore slow to bolt, making it harvestable over the longest season possible. Ready to pick in 45 days.

B 'BUTTERCRUNCH' is a heat-tolerant Bibb lettuce that forms a crunchy, yellow-white heart. It is notable for tender leaves that are tasty right into summer. Ready to pick in about 50 days.

C OAK LEAF varieties are heat-tolerant leaf lettuces excellent for sowing a second crop later in the summer. Try seeding some under the light shade of small trees. Ready to pick in 45 days.

D RED LEAF LETTUCES have attractive burgundy or deep maroon coloration that perks up any salad. Most varieties remain tender and flavorful as summer heats up and provide welcome contrasting color. Ready to pick in 50 days.

E SPECKLED LETTUCES are the latest rage (although at least one variety is thought to have been in cultivation since the 1700s). They are loose-leaf lettuces with crunchy, sweet, rounded green leaves attractively spotted and dotted with red. Most are ready to pick in 40 to 50 days.

There was a time not so long ago that lettuce meant only three or four varieties: Iceberg, Romaine, a ruffly looseleaf such as 'Black-seeded Simpson', and maybe butterhead or Bibb—all one shade of green or another. Now the variety is mind-boggling, with a seemingly never-ending stream of new varieties that have red leaves or green leaves with red edging, or vice versa. Some lettuces even have red-speckled leaves. Lettuces grow best in cool weather, in a range of temperatures from above freezing to about 60°F. However, breeders keep improving heat resistance, and some varieties are specifically recommended for growing in summer. For best results, plant several sowings of different lettuces at two-week intervals, beginning as soon as you can work the ground in spring and continuing to about May. Start again in early August for fall pickings. You can sow some lettuce as groundcover around small trees in big pots.

Lettuce 'Deer Tongue'

Lettuce 'Buttercrunch'

Lettuce 'Royal Oak Leaf'

Lettuce 'Red Fire'

Lettuce 'Bunte Forellenschluss'

Direct-Sowing Seeds

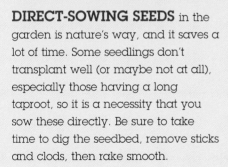

▲Before seedlings crowd one another for light and air, thin by hand or with floral scissors.

DIRECT-SOWING SEEDS in the garden is nature's way, and it saves a lot of time. Some seedlings don't transplant well (or maybe not at all), especially those having a long taproot, so it is a necessity that you sow these directly. Be sure to take time to dig the seedbed, remove sticks and clods, then rake smooth.

1 Finely rake and level a seedbed of good garden loam, then spread a ½- to 1-inch-deep layer of seed-starting mix over the surface.

2 To sow in a long row (called a drill), mark its length with garden stakes and twine pulled taut between. Open the drill with the edge of a hoe and add a ½- to 1-inch-deep layer of seed-starting mix in the bottom. Plant seeds in the drill, spacing them according to guidelines printed on the seed packet. If you sow too thickly, thinning later is a possibility but it can be tedious.

3 Cover the seeds with a ¼-inch layer of fine sand.

4 Water the seedbed with a fine mist. The sand helps stabilize the planting bed and can keep seeds in place even through hard rain.

"LARKSPUR AND POPPY are favorite candidates for direct seeding. If your garden gets snow, you can sow these and other hardy annuals and biennials directly on the snow."

—Peter Strauss

In this chapter

160 STORAGE THAT SHINES

Transform a dull prefab toolshed into a favorite destination with lattice and tree roses.

162 Plants: Favorite Tree Roses
163 Technique: Preparing Roses for Winter

164 A BEAUTIFUL HOME NURSERY

Turn your home nursery into a thing of beauty with display shelves made from prefabricated stair stringers.

166 Plants: Kitchen Plants
167 Technique: Plants from Pits and Seeds

168 INSTANT HOLDING BEDS WITH WATTLE

Create a raised holding bed for nursery pots or summering houseplants using the ancient craft of wattling.

170 Plants: Colorful Indoor-Outdoor Plants
171 Technique: Bringing Houseplants Indoors for the Winter

172 DRESSING UP A POTTING BENCH

Turn a standard potting bench into a decorative feature with a little lattice.

174 Equipment: Tools and Supplies for the Potting Bench
175 Technique: Reading Pest Control Labels

176 BUILDING A COLD FRAME

Multiply your plants in mini seedling and cutting nurseries. Tuck them between perennials and under shrubs, or use cold frames.

178 Plants: Plants Easy to Root from Cuttings
179 Technique: Making a Cutting

Gardens That Support

The success and satisfaction you get from your garden depends in part on the support facilities you have backstage. Most people take for granted that a cook or chef who serves up delicious food has a well-stocked kitchen and pantry. Gardeners, on the other hand, often attempt to cultivate beautiful gardens without convenient storage for supplies, worktables of appropriate height, or requisite tools at the ready. Also needed are growing and holding facilities that add up to a working home nursery. Having the support of your own garden work center is sure to make you a better, happier gardener.

Storage That Shines

Use lattice to transform an ordinary metal or wood shed into an attractive garden feature and add to its storage capacity in the process.

▲ Attach Lattice to Shed
Choose a color that complements the shed and its setting. Vinyl panels fit into vinyl brackets. They work well because they require little if any maintenance.

▲ Hang Tools by Grippers
Keep hand tools where they are within easy reach for yard and garden work and you can enjoy their appearance. Use large-size handle grippers to hang them.

▲ Plant Tree Roses in Pots
Place the bare roots of a tree rose on a mound of premium potting mix in an 18-inch pot. Cover with soil, filling pot.

If you already have one of these metal (or wood) storage sheds sitting out in your yard, it's probably packed with gardening tools, power equipment, a bike or two, toys, and anything else you can cram in. It might hold a chaotic mess that entails a wrestling match when you want to find and use something. On the other hand, if you don't already count a storage shed among your possessions, you will soon discover the potential of one.

Start with a basic metal or wood shed and prepare to transform it into a pretty garden house. Covering the exterior walls with sheets of vinyl lattice transforms the simple storage structure into an attractive garden feature. It will hold everything you need to maintain your yard and garden, keeping things neat and handy at the same time. Store large items inside the shed and hang hand tools on the exterior walls.

Reasonably priced prefab sheds are available at home centers in a variety of sizes and styles. You'll find the vinyl lattice panels and brackets in various colors there too. Place the shed where you will have easy access to it from anywhere in the yard, leaving room to move a lawn mower or snowblower in and out. Decorating the shed with lattice allows you to use it as a garden backdrop and to feel good about it being in plain view.

Materials and Equipment

- Prefab storage shed
- Vinyl lattice and brackets
- Handsaw or electric saw
- Screws; portable drill and screw bit
- Large S hooks or handle grippers; two 18" pots

The Plants
shown on the opposite page

- Two 36" patio tree roses ('Starry Night' is shown here)

Plan of Action

1 Place a storage shed in the yard where it will be convenient and attractive.
2 Measure the exterior walls of the shed. Purchase enough sheets of vinyl lattice and brackets to cover the two largest outside walls. You also can cover the back of the shed with lattice, if you desire.
3 Cut lattice to fit, if necessary, using a saw (hand or electric). Miter corners of brackets. Screw the brackets into place and insert lattice. Screw lattice to shed.
4 Add to the pleasant aesthetic of the shed's exterior: Hang a basket, a watering can, or other decorative items next to the strictly practical ones.
5 Pot tree roses and place them near the shed's entry. See page 163 for tips on how to protect tree roses over winter.

A nondescript, prefab tool shed serves its purpose by storing garden tools and equipment. But its ordinary looks become extraordinary with the addition of lattice, and by hanging garden tools on the outside like ornaments. Potted 'Starry Night' tree roses provide a finishing touch.

BEFORE

Favorite Tree Roses

A 'STARRY NIGHT' produces single, pure white blooms in large clusters throughout the season. The glossy-leaved plants are disease-resistant and the single blooms have an old-fashioned or wild-rose appearance.

B 'BONICA' was the first shrub rose to be named an All-America Rose Selection. It is cast-iron hardy (Zones 4 to 9) and everblooming. The apple-scented medium pink flowers are followed by orange seed hips in fall.

C 'GRAHAM THOMAS' is an English rose with tea rose fragrance. The cupped apricot flowers age to a soft creamy yellow. The foliage is glossy, bright green, and disease-resistant.

D 'KNOCK OUT' is notably hardy and produces raspberry red flowers. This new rose is causing a sensation among rose growers due to its complete resistance to disease. It has glossy blue-green leaves and blooms prolifically until frost.

E 'BLACK JADE' is a miniature rose with velvety, dark red (almost black) flowers and lustrous dark green leaves. It has only a hint of fragrance but is a prodigious bloomer.

TREE-FORM ROSES OUTSHINE most other garden stars, whether planted in the ground or in pots, especially where garden space is limited. Their upright forms provide head-high, eye-catching displays even when not in bloom. Those that are fragrant provide a treat for the senses at a most convenient height. Choose everblooming rose varieties that bloom throughout the growing season. You'll find standard tree forms of many favorite hybrid tea, floribunda, miniature, and shrub roses grafted onto 24-, 36-, or occasionally even 60-inch-tall trunks. The 18-inch standard miniature roses are ideal for small gardens and patios.

Tree roses need the same sunny location and biweekly feeding as other roses. Water weekly (or more if potted; daily in hottest weather). Trim the top periodically to keep it rounded. In late summer, stop feeding and cutting roses to encourage the plants to prepare for a winter rest. Protect tree roses during winter in any region where freezes occur (see opposite page).

Rosa 'Starry Night'

Rosa 'Bonica'

Rosa 'Graham Thomas'

Rosa 'Knock Out'

Rosa 'Black Jade'

Preparing Roses for Winter

Although some roses are hardier than others, all need winter protection in cold climates. Drying winds and fluctuating temperatures injure plants. With a little TLC in late fall, plants will survive and thrive for years. During winter months in warm climates, roses need a rest from growing and blooming. In this case, stop feeding and take a break from rose gardening until late winter when plants resume growing.

In cold climates, after the first frost when plants have stopped growing, protect hardy roses under a 12-inch-thick blanket of mulch. Pile it over the base of the plant. In the coldest climates, you can gently uproot the least hardy roses and tree roses with a garden fork. Lay them flat in a trench, then bury them under a 12-inch layer of mulch. Unearth them in spring and replant.

Tree roses need extra protection because their bud union is at the top

▲ In late fall or early winter, mound compost 12 inches high around the base of the rosebush and pile chopped leaves on top to protect the plant from winter's ravages. In early spring, gradually uncover the plant so light and air can reach the new shoots.

of the trunk. A relatively simple procedure can save them: Pot the tree rose (if it is not already potted) and move it to a garage or other space where temperatures stay above 20°F. Keep the soil moistened at the outset and make sure it remains damp throughout the winter.

Before winter, ▶ move tree roses to a sheltered location, such as an attached garage. Return tree roses to the garden when the tulips and daffodils are in bloom.

"PREPARING ROSES FOR WINTER CALLS FOR gauntlet gloves and determination to do battle. In really cold places, roses are generally cut back to knee height. Where I live in California they have to be forced to rest in late winter to ensure next year's roses won't be on a 15-foot stem!"

—Peter Strauss

Having a home nursery will make you a better gardener. It is most satisfying to have a place where you can line up newly potted seedlings and rooted cuttings for them to grow until they are ready to set into the garden.

A Beautiful Home Nursery

Build your own little stairway to heaven. This haven for plants gives you a place to coddle new acquisitions and grow your own supply of cuttings and divisions.

Call it a glorified plant shelf or a backstage holding area for young plants and wannabe bloomers that aren't quite ready for their turn to shine in the garden. Tucked away in a sometimes shady yard, and attached to a fence or outbuilding, it furnishes an ideal place to congregate outdoor potted plants and newly arrived nursery stock.

Any way you look at it, the wood stair-step structure provides an impressive 12 square feet of storage space for as many plants as you can set on the three steps. The heavy-duty slatted shelves allow water to run off, aiding drainage for the plants. The steps boost air circulation around the plants by holding them off the ground.

Prefabricated stringers (stair-step side and center pieces) make this project doable for novices. You won't want to climb these steps, but you do want them to be strong. Use nonrusting deck screws for the shelves, and coach or lag screws to hold the stringers to the back brace and to attach the back brace to the supporting structure. Have the 1×2s for the shelves precut at the lumberyard, and the project becomes mostly a matter of assembly. Build it with cedar for a structure that weathers well. Then seal it with clear sealer, or paint or exterior stain in a favorite color.

Materials and Equipment

- Three prefabricated 3-step stringers
- Twenty-one cedar 1×2s 8' long
- One 10' 2×4 cut to one 8' piece and three 6" pieces
- One 1-pound box galvanized or stainless steel 3" deck screws
- Saw; level; cordless drill

The Plants
shown on the opposite page

- New ones, old ones, fat ones, skinny ones, tall plants, short plants, pretty plants, sickly ones, green guys, and flowery treasures: You can bring any plant in a pot to your 3-step nursery.

Plan of Action

1 Place the horizontal back brace at an appropriate height on the supporting structure (fence or outbuilding), check level, and attach it.
2 Set 6-inch 2×4s under the bottom of each stringer to form a level base; secure them with screws. Place the two side stringers, check level, and attach them to the back brace with screws. Repeat with the center stringer.
3 Lay seven 1×2s across each step to form the shelves. Space the gaps equally between the slats, sliding a nail in and out between them. Screw the slats to the stringers.
4 Set up your plant nursery and watch everything grow.

▲ **Get on the Level**
An extra pair of hands can help with the initial building, such as leveling and mounting the back brace and installing the stringers on a 6-inch 2×4 block.

▲ **One Step at a Time**
Install the 1×2s one after the other and before you know it, the steps or shelves will be ready for plants. Spread an organic mulch to keep the area tidy.

▲ **Vacationing Kitchen Plants**
It's fun to grow potted plants from all kinds of seeds and pits salvaged from the kitchen: avocado, citrus, and papaya. They like to spend summer outdoors.

Kitchen Plants

A AVOCADO is fun to grow from the pit taken from a very ripe fruit. Set it in water to sprout with the tip exposed to light. Keep warm and moist. After two or three leaves form, transplant to a pot and pinch out the tip to encourage a bushy plant with numerous branches.

B MANGO is a tropical fruit with a large seed that you can plant and grow into an interesting specimen with glossy dark green leaves. The plant craves warmth and sunlight; avoid frosty windows and cold drafts.

C PINEAPPLE is started from the top of a ripe fruit. Cut off the leaf rosette leaving a little of the fruit at the base. Air-dry overnight, then snuggle the base into moist potting soil. Provide warmth and full sun. It will reach fruiting size in two years.

D LEMONGRASS is a tropical, clump-forming grass with lemon-flavor leaf bases. It grows easily in a big pot and reaches 3 to 5 feet tall in a sunny place with lots of water and warmth. Essential for Thai and Vietnamese cuisine.

E SWEET POTATO is a trailing plant that forms the familiar, edible, tuberous roots. Suspend in water by inserting toothpicks as shown, and grow in a warm, bright window in full sun.

TREASURE LIES IN YOUR KITCHEN trash or compost bucket. The potential for exotic houseplants is contained in the seeds, pits, and other seemingly useless parts of exotic edibles. Instead of tossing them, consider growing the plants noted at left, along with many others that are easy and entertaining to raise from seed. Citrus fruits, ginger, date, pomegranate, passionfruit, and more have potential for a kitchen windowsill garden. Sometimes these plants require a little patience as you wait for them to sprout, but you'll enjoy the added satisfaction of keeping them going from year to year. This is a great project for budding gardeners, especially youngsters. Provide seeds and seedlings with sunlight, warmth, and consistent moisture. You will not harvest fruit from an avocado or mango you're growing in your window. This is for growing fun and adventure!

Avocado

Mango

Pineapple

Lemongrass

Sweet potato

Plants from Pits and Seeds

▲ Take an avocado pit from a ripe fruit. Do not cut the seed. Support on toothpicks, with the tip exposed, in a glass of water. When it sprouts, transplant to potting mix in a container. Give it full sun and warmth.

▲ Citrus seeds of all kinds sprout readily if they are taken from a very ripe fruit. Plant in moist potting mix ½ inch deep; grow in a warm, sunny place.

A sunny kitchen windowsill makes an ideal place to nurture seedlings. The warmth and humidity of the location bolsters new plant growth. It also makes it easy for you to check on the moisture needs of the fledgling plants as part of your daily routine. If your kitchen lacks exposure to bright light, keep plants under a fluorescent grow-light that can be plugged into a timer to automatically provide "days" of 16 hours duration (see page 82).

To grow a pineapple, start with a healthy leaf rosette from the top of a ripe pineapple. Slice off the leaf rosette with an inch of core attached. Peel off three or four lower leaves. Let dry overnight or up to two days. Set to root in moist seed starting mix. Keep warm in bright light. When the leaves start to grow, transplant to moist potting soil.

Pomegranate seeds sprout easily if you take them from a ripe fruit. Cover with moist potting soil to the depth of their own thickness and set to sprout and grow in a sunny, warm window garden.

> **"ANY SEED THAT COMES INTO THE KITCHEN** and has not been cooked, pickled, or irradiated is fair game for growing—mostly for fun, rarely for fruit."
>
> —Peter Strauss

TO GROW A MANGO, START WITH A RIPE FRUIT.

1 Remove as much flesh from around the seed as possible.

2 Soak the seed in water for two to three days.

3 After the tough outer husk has softened, pry it open and remove the inner seed. Plant it to the depth of its own thickness in moist seed-starting mix. Place in a warm spot; the seed usually germinates in three to four weeks.

Instant Holding Beds with Wattle

Wattle, a structure interwoven with slender branches, gives gardeners a way to turn yard waste into building materials. The technique is as easy as child's play.

The garden bed frame shown has a long-standing historical precedent. Wattle fences have been woven around gardens since medieval times. Rounded or squared enclosures made of bendable prunings serve as a holding area for newly acquired plants that await planting. They also can showcase houseplants that are summering outdoors.

The display idea shown was inspired by a technique used at flower shows. An especially colorful or floriferous arrangement looks pretty enough to serve as a centerpiece for a party in the yard. Set the plants inside the ring, arranging the tallest ones in the center. Raise a pot, if necessary, by propping it up on a brick.

The 12-inch high, 48-inch-wide construction requires weaving skills along the lines of what you learned in kindergarten while making baskets or paper placemats.

Gather fresh-cut prunings, such as red-twig dogwood, crape myrtle, or willow branches. Lengths of ¼- to ½-inch-thick green wood are the most supple. Dead wood will crack and break. If you don't plan to do any pruning soon, keep an eye out for neighbors' trimmings discarded at the curb. One way or the other, this is a perfect way to use materials otherwise destined for a landfill or compost pile.

Materials and Equipment

- Pruner, hand or long-handled
- Fifty prunings 4' to 6' long
- Garden hose
- Eighteen bamboo stakes 18" long
- Hammer
- Eighteen 2" clay pots

The Plants
shown on the page opposite

- One 5-gallon bougainvillea standard (tree)
- Four 3-gallon gold-leaved hostas
- Four 1-gallon apricot *Ixora*
- Four 1-gallon 'Stargazer' lilies
- Four 6" double white impatiens
- Four 6" pink pentas
- Four 6" dark purple *Plectranthus*

Plan of Action

1. Determine where you will make the enclosure. Use a garden hose to lay out a 4-foot-diameter circle.
2. Pound the bamboo stakes into the ground about 9 inches apart to form the circle of uprights.
3. Trim off any side branches or leaves from the long prunings to make them as sleek as possible.
4. Take a long branch and weave it in and out; continue around the circle, one layer at a time. After a while, push down several layers so little space is left between. Continue to almost the top of the vertical canes.
5. As a finishing touch, place a little clay pot upside down on top of each cane. The effect is both decorative and practical, the latter to avoid poking an eye.

▲ **Wattling is Basket-Weaving** Use fresh-cut green prunings, saplings, or grapevines for weaving in and out between vertical sticks or bamboo canes driven into the ground at 9-inch intervals.

▲ **Pots Protect Eyes and Look Good** Small clay pots placed over the vertical bamboo stakes provide a charming feature as well as increased safety. Small colored-glass bottles are attractive too.

▲ **Staging the Plant Show** Bricks placed under some of the pots raise the pots into ascending order.

Old-fashioned wattling woven from spring prunings encircles this holding bed to make it an attractive focal point in the garden. Newly purchased nursery stock can be displayed here until there is time to plant it in the garden. Tiny pots add a whimsical finishing touch.

Colorful Indoor-Outdoor Plants

A PURPLE PLECTRANTHUS is an exceptional new plant that grows enthusiastically all summer in sun to partial shade and blooms in the fall. It boasts dark green leaves with purple undersides and lavender-blue flowers.

B JUNGLE FLAME is a tropical that blooms nonstop in warmth and sun with ample water. Feed with plant food for acid-loving plants and keep the soil evenly moist. Colors include pink, red, and orange.

C JASMINE comes in many varieties. *Jasminum polyanthum* (shown) is often sold in winter or spring trained as a wreath. It needs a cool, sunny window. 'Maid of Orleans' is everblooming and a choice plant for any warm, sunny spot.

D BROMELIAD is the popular name for ornamental members of the pineapple family. They thrive in bright light and high humidity. Keep the leaf cups filled with fresh water.

E HYDRANGEA comes in many varieties, some hardy. The tender florist types can live in Zone 6 gardens and warmer. Elsewhere they need wintering over in a cool window with barely moist soil. Repot in spring, provide half sun, and feed frequently with plant food for acid-loving plants.

PERENNIALLY POPULAR INDOOR-OUTDOOR garden rooms call for a broad palette of versatile plants with colorful foliage and flowers. When grouped, such plants create an instant garden setting in the house or on a patio, deck, balcony, or porch. Depend on these plants to make an impact, whether their color is seasonal, or strong year-round. On the whole, colorful plants brighten the dreariest days, setting a cheerful tone in a room and making outstanding focal points. Each of these colorful plants has other qualities that make it desirable. Some offer fragrance, others need little maintenance. Unlike annuals that put on a bright show for a limited time and die, or perennials that bloom year after year mainly in the garden, these plants cover all the bases. They live on as long as you tend to their basic needs and keep them from freezing. Look for other candidates among the summer tropicals.

Plectranthus hillardiae

Ixora longifolia

Jasminum polyanthum

Neoregelia carolinea meyendorfii 'Albomarginata'

Hydrangea macrocarpa 'Kluis Superba'

Bringing Houseplants Indoors for the Winter

▲ Before bringing indoors a plant that has summered outside, check the leaf undersides and along the stems for signs of mealybug, scale, or spider mites.

▲ If unwanted insects are detected, spray with a pest control labeled specifically for use on houseplants and the type of insect you have detected.

▲ Before a killing frost, dig summer bulbs and tubers from the garden and store them in peat. Or, if they are in pots, bring the pots inside. Bulbs and tubers that should be wintered indoors include calla lilies, *Eucomis, Ismene, Oxalis,* rain lilies, *Caladium,* elephant ear (*Colocasia*), *Gladiolus,* and *Dahlia.* Put them in an attached garage or any storage room where temperatures stay well above freezing. When the leaves have died away, remove them. If the bulbs are not labeled, be sure to add identification tags; otherwise it will be potluck next growing season.

P lants like to take summer vacations too. When placed outdoors under a tree or in a protected corner of a patio, many houseplants benefit from filtered light and refreshing showers. Ordinary foliage plants as well as dwarf citrus, jasmine, flowering maple, and other flowering tropicals display renewed vigor and beauty. In fall, when temperatures begin to drop in all but the mildest climates, they must be brought back indoors to spend the winter.

Move other plants into the house for the winter that began life in the summer garden and are too tender to remain outdoors. Return them to the garden come spring. Potted herbs, such as rosemary, lemon verbena, and parsley, respond well to this treatment.

All plants that do the indoor-outdoor shuffle need an inspection and grooming before moving indoors. Otherwise insect pests may hitchhike into a cozy environment where they can spread to other plants. Examine each plant for signs of pests. Look at all sides of the

▲ Indoors, quarantine plants that have been outdoors, such as this croton, keeping them away from other plants until you're certain they are free of insects.

leaves and stems; poke around in the soil. Clues of problems include yellowing leaves, webs where leaves meet stems, stickiness on leaves, insects hopping out of the soil, and specks clinging to the leaves or moving on them. Give your plants a thorough shower and an insect control treatment before moving them indoors (follow the steps shown above).

"HOUSEPLANTS THAT SPEND THE SUMMER outdoors almost always grow bigger—sometimes a lot bigger. Assess, measure, and prune if need be. It's a good idea to get houseplants back indoors a couple of weeks before turning on the heat."

—Peter Strauss

It may look ▶
depressingly
industrial, but this
bench from an
inexpensive kit
has promise.

BEFORE

Dressing Up a Potting Bench

Transform an affordable workbench into a potting center with appeal by encasing it in pine slats. Outfit it for efficient use and safe storage of tools and supplies.

Chances are, you'll be so pleased with the finished look and handiness of this potting bench, it could be moved from the garage or garden shed into your home. It might be an ideal desk for the home office or a funky china cupboard for the dining room. But first, try it as a place to keep your potting supplies and small gardening gear.

This bench provides convenient places to pot plants, hang essential potting tools, and store containers of soil and amendments. It even includes a lockable cupboard for storing pest controls and plant foods, keeping them high, dry, and out of the reach of children and pets.

A ready-made workbench, assembled from a kit and available at building centers or from catalog suppliers, forms the basis for this design. The workbench pictured includes a pegboard and a drawer. The dressed-up, 74×48-inch bench includes an added top shelf and upper cupboard. This bench is suited as an indoor work area. If you prefer a more weather-worthy model for outdoor use, shop for a cedar bench and select cedar to trim it.

Encasing the bench with pine slats takes a little time to measure, plan, cut, and fasten. Cut all the wood at a 90-degree angle. Build the upper portion of the structure first, then attach the sidepieces.

▲ Pine Slats Can Transform
Pine verticals give the bench another dimension, and garden style.

▲ From Work to Garden Bench
Leave the finished bench natural, or seal, stain, or paint it to your liking.

▲ A Lock Ensures Safety
A small padlock on the cupboard door is a good child-proofing idea if you plan on storing sharp tools or pest controls.

Materials and Equipment

- One workbench kit 48¾" wide × 24½" deep × 36" tall (57" tall at back shelf). If yours varies in size, adjust the dimensions that follow.
- Eighteen 1×2s 8' long, cut into eight 74" lengths (rear sides); ten 37¼" lengths (front sides); eighteen 19" lengths (cupboard door uprights); four 23¼" lengths (cupboard door horizontals); two 22" lengths (top ends of table); two 23" lengths (side horizontals); two 8½" lengths (side horizontals of top shelf); and one 48⅞" length (top shelf horizontal support)
- One 1×10 shelf 50¼" long
- ½ pound 1½" drywall screws
- Four 1½" hinges
- One 1½" safety latch
- Drill and saw

Plan of Action

1. Start with an assemble-yourself workbench kit (available at most home centers).
2. Measure the workbench, plan the design, then buy the wood to trim the workbench according to the one shown or adapting to suit your need.
3. Cut the wood.
4. Assemble the wood shell and secure it to the workbench. Attach hardware for cupboard doors, including the hinges and latch. Install cupboard doors.
5. Outfit the potting bench, including hooks to hang small tools on the pegboard. Mount storage baskets on the sides of the structure.

Tools and Supplies
For the Potting Bench

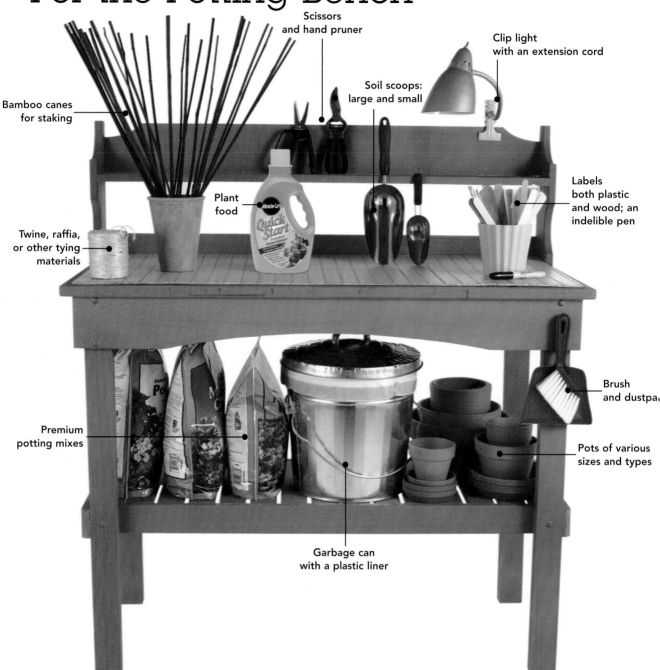

Bamboo canes for staking

Scissors and hand pruner

Clip light with an extension cord

Soil scoops: large and small

Plant food

Labels both plastic and wood; an indelible pen

Twine, raffia, or other tying materials

Premium potting mixes

Brush and dustpan

Pots of various sizes and types

Garbage can with a plastic liner

WHETHER YOU PLAN TO transplant seedlings or repot large plants, you need an efficient work space where you can keep all the important tools and supplies. A well-equipped potting bench keeps your essential paraphernalia organized, within easy reach, and tidy. If your potting bench includes a small sink or other source of water, it will help make cleanup a breeze. If not, situate your potting bench near a faucet. A bench with shelves above and below the work surface, such as the one shown above, makes an efficient arrangement. The most indispensable tools and supplies for potting are shown. Change the organization depending on the methods you prefer and the layout of your bench. Perhaps you'd like a place to store seeds or your garden journal. Keep a stool handy to sit on while you work. And remember: don't put an item down, put it away.

Reading Pest Control Labels

Pest controls offered at retail stores almost invariably do what they claim on the label and—if precautions are followed—with little danger to humans, pets, and wildlife. Problems can occur from a failure to read and comprehend exactly what the label claims and instructs. An insecticide states specifically which insects it controls and the number of treatments needed to be effective. A fungicide states specifically what diseases it controls and on which plants. A herbicide states which weeds (monocotyledons such as grass or dicotyledons such as dandelion) it controls. It is important to know the difference between insecticides, fungicides, and herbicides.

The main front label tells the type of plant (rose and flower), usage (insect killer), and active ingredient(s). This one offers the convenience of being for both garden and houseplant use.

The main back label states which insects can be treated with the product, where (indoors or outdoors), and on what type of plants it may be used.

Always store pesticides under lock and key and dispose of them only as indicated on the label.

Always read the precautionary statements before applying any pest control.

A peel-back feature permits more details on how best to apply, when to apply, specific insects controlled, storage and disposal directions, and precautions.

It's liberating to be creative in the garden, but not in terms of how and when to apply a pest control. Follow the directions.

Not every insecticide is licensed for controlling every insect or is even effective in controlling every insect. Use an insecticide only against the insect(s) listed on the label.

The universal symbol for the telephone tells you that the number to call for more information or help is right here.

DIRECTIONS FOR USE
It is a violation of Federal law to use this product in a manner inconsistent with its labeling.
SHAKE WELL

FOR BEST RESULTS

HOW TO APPLY
- Adjust spray nozzle to deliver a fine spray.
- Hold sprayer 12 inches from plant. Spray to uniformly cover upper and lower leaf surfaces, stems, and branches. When treating potted plants lightly spray the soil surface.

WHEN TO APPLY
- Spray when air is calm to avoid drift.
- Apply as necessary, waiting 7 to 14 days between each application. Hard to kill insects may require 2 to 3 applications.
- If temperature is expected to exceed 85° F, spray in early morning or late afternoon when it is cooler.

INSECTS CONTROLLED
Ants, aphids, armyworms, bagworms, black vine weevils, budworms, cabbage loopers, cankerworms, casebearers, catalpa sphinx moths, caterpillars, cherry laurel leaftiers, crane flies, elm leaf beetles, fungus gnats, grasshoppers, greenbugs, green striped mapleworms, gypsy moths, hornworms, Japanese beetles, lacebugs, leafhoppers, leafminers, leafrollers, omnivorous leaftiers, maple shoot moths, mealybugs, mimosa webworms, mites (including spider mites), oak webworm, orange striped oakworms, poplar tentmakers, rose midges, sawflies, scales (crawlers), seed webworms, sowbugs, spittlebugs, spiders, sunflower moths, tent caterpillars, thrips, tip moths, webworms, weevils, willow leafbeetles and whiteflies.

People and pets may enter treated area after spray has dried.

STORAGE AND DISPOSAL
STORAGE: Rotate nozzle to closed position. Store product in original container in a safe place. Keep from freezing.
DISPOSAL: Do not reuse container. Securely wrap partially filled or empty container in newspaper and put in trash.

PRECAUTIONARY STATEMENTS
HAZARDS TO HUMANS & DOMESTIC ANIMALS
CAUTION: Causes moderate eye irritation. Avoid contact with eyes or clothing. Wash thoroughly with soap and water after handling.
FIRST AID: IF IN EYES: Flush eyes with plenty of water. Call a physician if irritation persists. **Note to Physician:** Emergency Information call 1-800-225-2883.
ENVIRONMENTAL HAZARDS: This pesticide is extremely toxic to fish and aquatic invertebrates. Do not apply directly to water. Drift and run-off from treated areas may be hazardous to aquatic organisms in neighboring areas. Care should be used when spraying to avoid fish and reptile pets in/around ornamental ponds.
This product is highly toxic to bees exposed to direct treatment or residues on blooming plants. Do not apply this product or allow it to drift to blooming plants if bees are visiting the treatment area.
NOTICE: Buyer assumes all responsibility for safety and use not in accordance with directions.

Questions, Comments or Medical Information call 1-800-225-2883 www.ortho.com

Manufactured for
The ORTHO Group
P.O. Box 1749 Columbus, OH 43216
Made in USA

Form 008900
EPA Reg. No. 239-2668
EPA Est. 239-IA-3[1], 56100-LA-1[G]
Superscript is first letter of lot number

PRESS TO RESEAL

Building a Cold Frame

When you build a cold frame and add it to your garden, you'll wonder how you ever got along without one. It opens up all kinds of options to grow better plants.

Use a cold frame to nurture young plants as they grow big enough for life in the garden. Seedlings and cuttings need protection from harsh weather in spring and fall.

A cold frame helps to extend the growing season both at its beginning and at its end, which is especially important if you live in a region where the time for gardening outdoors is limited. Situated on the sunny side of a house and insulated with styrene sheets cut to line the box, a cold frame allows cold-climate gardeners to grow lettuce and other greens through the winter.

You can easily build a cold frame in a weekend. Ready-made options are also available. Possibilities for more low-tech versions include making a box frame and covering it with an old window sash, and setting up bales of straw or concrete blocks and laying the glass over the frame. Add a heating cable or drip irrigation to make it even more useful.

The ideal cold frame has sloped sides and a top that you can open and close to give plants the light and air they need. The bottom is open so you can set the frame on an existing garden or a bed of sand, water freely, and move it around the yard.

Warm the cold frame on coldest days by stacking bales of hay or straw around it. Shade on warmest days with bamboo or reed fencing.

▲ Build It to Last
Plastic sleeves with mitered corners edge the cover. The plastic cover is screwed to a wood frame and metal braces.

▲ Start with the Best Materials
Build a cold frame using simple building plans, weather-resistant cedar for the frame, and heavy-duty but lightweight greenhouse plastic for the cover.

Materials and Equipment

- For the box. Cedar lumber: three 7/8"×12"×48" pieces (front and rear); three 7/8"×12"×44¾" pieces, one cut in half diagonally into same-size wedges (sides); four 2"×2"×21" pieces; two 2"×2"×15" pieces; two 2"×2"×10" pieces (braces)
- Two 2½" utility hinges

- For the cover. Cedar lumber: two 7/8"×3"×48" pieces; three 7/8"×3"×43" pieces Four 6" flat-corner braces
- Two 4"×4" T braces
- 48"×48" piece of polycarbonate twinwall greenhouse glazing
- Four 48" plastic sleeves
- Screws with rubber washers

Plan of Action

1 Lay out lumber and cut pieces as shown on the opposite page.
2 Assemble the box using 2-inch wood screws. Position shortest braces at the front, tallest at the back.
3 Assemble the top. Place hardware on the bottom side and set toward the inside of the frame so it will fit snugly on the box. When complete, attach top to bottom using two 2½-inch utility hinges. To install the polycarbonate glazing on the frame, use the screws with rubber washers. Miter the corners for the plastic sleeves (using hack saw) and slide in place.
4 Place the cold frame so it will be oriented from east to west. Slightly sink the frame into the ground, to secure it and to use the earth as insulation.

▲ Maximize Sun and Fresh Air
Make the front of the frame lower than the other sides. On warm days, prop open the cold frame's cover and secure against the wind.

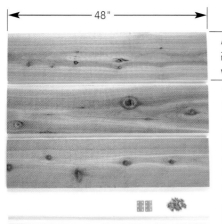

Three ⅞"×12"×48" boards, one for front, two (stacked) for back, and two 2½" utility hinges; screws with rubber washers built in for attaching polycarbonate glazing; four plastic sleeves that go around the glazing.

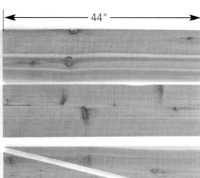

Two 44" pieces for the side panels.

The third 44-inch piece cut diagonally to sloping sides. Four 2"×2"×21", two 2"×2"×15", and two 2"×2"×10" for bracing interior walls.

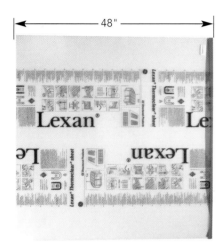

One 48-inch square of polycarbonate twinwall greenhouse glazing that lets warmth of sunlight in but doesn't let it out.

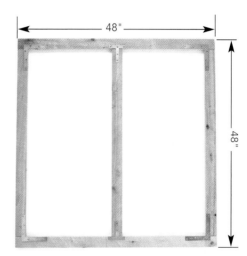

Two ⅞"×3"×48" pieces; three ⅞"×3"×43" pieces; four 6" flat corner braces and two 4"×4" T braces.

A small coldframe like this one is the sign of a good gardener. It gives a place to root special cuttings and to winter over prize seedlings. You can also grow an early, early crop of salad greens at the dawn of the new growing season.

Plants Easy to Root from Cuttings

A COLEUS is one of the easiest of all plants to root from cuttings. Cut or break off a vigorous tip cutting 4 to 5 inches long. Insert cutting in moist seed starting potting mix to root, or in a glass of water.

B ENGLISH IVY is fun to root, first in a glass of water, then transplanted to a pot of seed starting potting mix. Make the cutting immediately below a leaf. Strip off that leaf, and roots will grow there.

C AFRICAN VIOLET is one of those special plants that can grow from a leaf cutting. Cut a vigorous, middle-aged leaf (not the youngest, not the oldest on the plant). Insert the base of the cutting in moist seed starting potting mix to root. New plants will show in a few weeks.

D CHRYSANTHEMUM cuttings taken in spring from growth about 3 inches tall will root readily in seed starting potting mix and grow into plants stronger than those that sprout from old, established clumps.

E BOXWOOD can be started from semi-hardwood cuttings taken in late summer or fall. The cuttings should be firm enough to snap if bent sharply. Insert in moist seed starting mix and keep in cool, bright light.

Take cuttings of plants, also called slips, to expand your plant collection. Propagating methods include cutting a green stem piece, a hard woody piece, a single leaf, a bud, or a clump of roots. Most plants respond best to one or more of these methods. Generally the easiest and most common methods entail taking softwood (green stem) cuttings in spring, summer, or early fall or hardwood (pencil-size, woody stem) cuttings in autumn. Whichever stem-cutting method you use, cut a 4- to 6-inch growing end of a plant just below a node (where a leaf emerges), using a clean, sharp pruner, a knife, floral scissors, or razor blade. Follow the guidelines shown on the next page to complete the process. Some plants, such as chrysanthemums, grow best from cuttings, whereas their mother plant benefits from being cut apart and divided.

Making a Cutting

▲ Cuttings inclined to wilt badly when they are first set to root are given a better chance of survival when they are covered with a clear plastic bag (such as from the dry cleaner's) held in place with a bent wire clothes hanger. As soon as the leaves perk up, remove the plastic, at first for an hour or two, gradually increasing time until the cover is no longer needed.

SCENTED GERANIUMS

Pelargonium hybrids are among the easiest plants to grow from stem cuttings. Make cuttings anytime and, within months, enjoy pots of new plants or share them with your friends.

1 Cut a stem of a plant just below a leaf or leaf node (where a new leaf will develop). Pinch off the bottom leaves and any flowers, and buds. Also pinch off the papery stipules (appendages) at the base of the stem, because they can cause rot.

2 Sprinkle powdered rooting hormone into a saucer. Dip the cutting's end into the powder.

3 Use a pencil to form a planting hole in a small pot of premoistened starter mix. Slide the cutting into the hole without knocking off the rooting hormone.

Set the cutting to root in a warm but protected place, such as a bright window or a cold frame. Protect from intense midday sun. Add water only to prevent severe drying out of the planting mix.

4 After a few weeks, the roots will have taken hold and the cutting will show signs of vigorous new growth. Now is the time to transplant to a larger pot, usually one about 5 inches in diameter, filling in around the starter mix and new roots with new premium potting mix. Place in a warm, sunny window or garden.

"THAT A PLANT CAN GROW A COPY OF ITSELF from a cutting will never cease to amaze me. If a cutting has big floppy leaves, you can help reduce shock and encourage rooting by cutting off one-half to two-thirds of the leaf."

—Peter Strauss

USDA Plant Hardiness Zone Map

This map of climate zones helps you select plants for your garden that will survive a typical winter in your region. The United States Department of Agriculture (USDA) developed the map, basing the zones on the lowest recorded temperatures across North America. Zone 1 is the coldest area and Zone 11 is the warmest area.

Plants are classified by the coldest temperature and zone they can endure. For example, plants hardy to Zone 6 survive where winter temperatures drop to −10°F. Those hardy to Zone 8 die long before it's that cold. These plants may grow in colder regions but must be replaced each year. Plants rated for a range of hardiness zones can usually survive winter in the coldest region as well as tolerate the summer heat of the warmest one.

To find your hardiness zone, note the approximate location of your community on the map, then match the color band marking that area to the key.

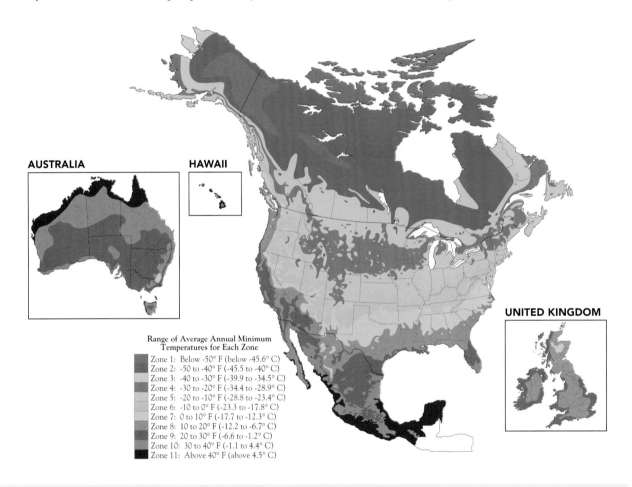

AUSTRALIA

HAWAII

UNITED KINGDOM

Range of Average Annual Minimum
Temperatures for Each Zone

Zone 1: Below -50° F (below -45.6° C)
Zone 2: -50 to -40° F (-45.5 to -40° C)
Zone 3: -40 to -30° F (-39.9 to -34.5° C)
Zone 4: -30 to -20° F (-34.4 to -28.9° C)
Zone 5: -20 to -10° F (-28.8 to -23.4° C)
Zone 6: -10 to 0° F (-23.3 to -17.8° C)
Zone 7: 0 to 10° F (-17.7 to -12.3° C)
Zone 8: 10 to 20° F (-12.2 to -6.7° C)
Zone 9: 20 to 30° F (-6.6 to -1.2° C)
Zone 10: 30 to 40° F (-1.1 to 4.4° C)
Zone 11: Above 40° F (above 4.5° C)

METRIC CONVERSIONS

U.S. Units to Metric Equivalents			Metric Units to U.S. Equivalents		
To Convert From	Multiply By	To Get	To Convert From	Multiply By	To Get
Inches	25.4	Millimeters	Millimeters	0.0394	Inches
Inches	2.54	Centimeters	Centimeters	0.3937	Inches
Feet	30.48	Centimeters	Centimeters	0.0328	Feet
Feet	0.3048	Meters	Meters	3.2808	Feet
Yards	0.9144	Meters	Meters	1.0936	Yards

To convert from degrees Fahrenheit (F) to degrees Celsius (C), first subtract 32, then multiply by ⅝.

To convert from degrees Celsius to degrees Fahrenheit, multiply by ⅖, then add 32.

First and Last Frost Dates

These maps indicate the average dates for the first and last frosts across North America. Many factors influence the accuracy of these dates. For example, at the bottom of a north-facing hill, spring comes later and fall earlier than on the top of the hill. Your local cooperative extension service can provide a more precise date for your location.

Light frosts occur when the temperature falls below 33° F. Light frost rarely poses a threat to cool-season annuals, such as pansies and ornamental cabbage, which grow quite well in cold weather in spring and fall.

Warm-season annuals are more variable. Some quickly succumb to light frost, whereas others, such as petunias, survive until a hard frost (around 28°F) knocks them down. However, it's best to wait until after the last frost in spring to set out warm-season annuals in the garden, and to rely on cool-season annuals to provide fall bloom.

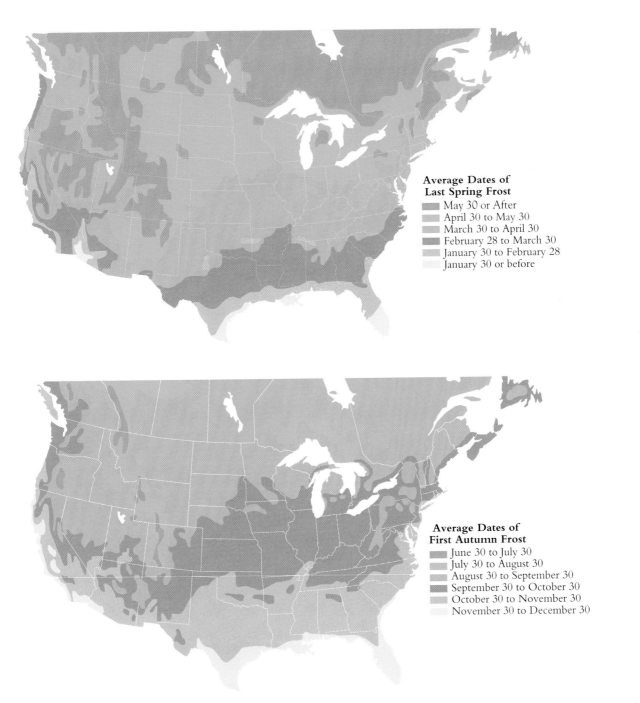

**Average Dates of
Last Spring Frost**
May 30 or After
April 30 to May 30
March 30 to April 30
February 28 to March 30
January 30 to February 28
January 30 or before

**Average Dates of
First Autumn Frost**
June 30 to July 30
July 30 to August 30
August 30 to September 30
September 30 to October 30
October 30 to November 30
November 30 to December 30

Resources for Plants and Supplies

Nearly everything used in the projects created for this book is readily available at your local home center, garden center, nursery, and hardware store. The few items that might need to be purchased through the mail or the internet are listed below.

Japanese bamboo fence: www.japanesegifts.com

If you can't find bamboo to build fencing and trellising: at local nurseries, garden centers, home improvement centers, it is available through mail order at Frank's Cane and Rush Supply, 7252 Heil Ave., Huntington Beach, CA 92647; 714/847-0707

Rain chain to use above a rain barrel: www.RainChains.com

Rain barrels can be ordered through www.Rainbarrelsandmore.com

Potting bench kit from Tidewater Workshop, 1515 Grant St., Egg Harbor City, NJ 98215; www.tidewaterworkshop.com

Double-wall polycarbonate greenhouse glazing used for the cold frame is available from Charley's Greenhouse and Garden Supplies. It is also a helpful catalog source for a host of other indoor plant supplies, including for growing orchids and African violets. www.charleysgreenhouse.com

Straps and stakes for newly planted trees are available from A.M. Leonard, www.amleo.com

To diagnose plant problems as early as possible, refer to *Ortho's Home Gardener's Problem Solver*, available wherever books are sold.

Hanging baskets, wrought-iron racks, and coir liners are available from the Kinsman Company, P.O. Box 428, Pipersville, PA 18947; www.kinsmangarden.com

Miracle-Gro® www.miracle-gro.com

For more information on how to garden successfully, go to www.miracle-gro.com where you'll find:

- **Email Reminder Service:** Free gardening tips and reminders sent to you via email

- **More Gardening Tips from Peter Strauss**

- **More Exciting Project Ideas**

- **Miracle-Gro Product Consumer Guide:** The latest information on all Miracle-Gro products, including plant foods, soil mixes, plants, and exciting new product lines from Miracle-Gro.

- **Garden Problem Solver:** Link into a comprehensive library of diagnostic tools and solutions for insect, disease, and weed problems.

- **Streaming How-to Videos:** Click into a library of more than 50 quick gardening and lawn care video clips

Index

Note: Page references in *italic type* indicate photographs or illustrations, and information in captions.

A

Abutilon. See Maple, flowering
Acer palmatum. See Maple, Japanese
Achillea. See Yarrow
Acorus, 78
Adiantum pedatum, 56
African violet, *84*
    making cuttings, 178, *178*
    profile, 84
    tips for growing, 82–84
Agave, 96
Ageratum
    'Blue Horizon', *144*
    profile, 144
Aglaonema. See Chinese evergreen
Air-conditioners
    cleaning, 72
    hiding, 72, *73*
Ajuga, 90
Allium schoenoprasum. See Chives
Aloe vera, 96, *96*
Aloysia triphylla. See Lemon verbena
Amaryllis, 106, *107, 109*
Anethum graveolens. See Dill
Annual plants. *See* Bedding plants
Anthoxanthum odoratum. See Sweet vernal
    grass
Antirrhinum. See Snapdragon
Aphids, *101*, 147
Apple (*Malus*)
    CrimsonSpire, 90, 92, *92*
    EmeraldSpire, 90, 92, *92*
    ScarletSpire, 90, 92, *92*
    UltraSpire, 90, 92, *92*
Arbors
    to frame views, 90, *91*
    garden gate upgrade, *32*, 33
    light-colored, 69
    rose, 20–23
Arborvitae (*Thuja*), 51, *74*
    profiles, 52, 74
    T. occidentalis 'Filiformis', *52*
Aster, dwarf, 46
Astilbe, 61
Avocado
    growing from seed, *167*
    profile, 166
Azalea pots, *15*

B

Baby's breath (*Gysophila paniculata*)
    'Bristol Fairy', *62*
    profile, 62
Back door makeover, 24–25
Backyard getaway, 46–47

Bacopa, 116
    profile, 30
    'Snowstorm', *30*
Bamboo plants
    in containers, 38–39
    profile, *40*
Bamboo screens
    front porch trellis, 42–43
    to hide air conditioners, *72*
    no-dig hedge, 38–39
Banana, edible flowers, 122
Bare-root roses, planting, 23
Bark, as mulch, 53
Basil (*Ocimum basilicum*), 54, *138*, 139
    'Spicy Globe', 113, 114, *114*
Bay, sweet (*Laurus nobilis*), 48, *48*
Beans
    bush, 136
    bush, 'Maxibel Filet', *136*
    pole, 140
    pole, 'Blue Lake', *140*
Bedding plants
    for backyard getaway, 46, *47*
    as centerpieces, 124–125
    for curbside flowers, 17, *18*
    for garden room oasis, 54
    for large container plantings,
        128–130
    planting, 127
    summer all-stars, profiles, 126
Begonia (*Begonia*)
    angel-wing, *90*
    'Dragon Wings', *28*, 130, *130*
    as houseplants, 82
    pots for, 15
    rex (*B. rex-cultorem*), 56
    rex (*B. rex-cultorem*) 'Escargot', *56*
    tuberous (*B.* x *tuberhybrida*), 109, 122
    tuberous (*B.* x *tuberhybrida*)
        'Nonstop Scarlet', *122*
    wax (*B. semperflorens-cultorem*), *125*,
        126
Benches, *50*, 51
Birdbaths, *68*, 116–*117*
Bleeding heart (*Dicentra*), 69
Blue oat grass (*Helictotrichon sempervirens*)
    profile, 62
    'Sapphire', *62*
Bog gardens, 78
bottle-glass mat, *32–33*
Bougainvillea (*Bougainvillea spectabilis*),
    44, *44*
Bower of flowers, *50–53*
Boxwood, making cuttings, 178, *178*
Brassica oleracea. See Kale, ornamental

Bromeliads
    Neoregelia carolinea meyendorfii
        'Albomarginata', *170*
    pineapple, *166,* 167
    profile, 170
Bulbs
    for curbside flowers, 17
    deadheading, 115
    growing lettuce with, 155
    for indoor blooms, 106–109
    overwintering indoors, *171*
    pots for, 15
Bunny ears (*Opuntia*), *96*
Buying plants
    bare-root roses, 23
    orchids, 103
    sun and shade preferences, 57
    tropical foliage plants, 26

C

Cacti and succulents
    caring for, 97
    garden on a wall, *94–95*, 97
    gravel mulches, *79*
    as houseplants, 95
    lighting for, *85*, 97
    pots for, 15
    profiles, 96
Cactus
    barrel, 96
    crown, 96
    golden ball, 96
    holiday (*Schlumbergera bridgesii*), 84,
        84
Caladium, *90*
    planting and growing, 109
    'Postman Joyner', *30*
    profile, 30
Calamagrostis acutiflora. See Feather reed
    grass
Calamondin (*Fortunella margarita*)
    'Nagami', *148*
    profile, 148
Calendula (*Calendula officinalis*)
    cut flowers, 144
    edible flowers, 113
    'Gitana', *114*
    profile, 114
Calibrachoa, 12, *13,* 98, *99,* 116
    profile, 100
    'Trailing Pink', *100*
Calla lily (*Zantedeschia rehmannii violacea*)
    'California Calla', *108*
    planting and growing, 109
    profile, 108
Candles, birdbath holder, 116–117
Carex pendula. See Sedge, drooping

Carrot
    profile, 136
    'Thumbelina', *136*
Cascading plants
    for container towers, 98, *99*
    foliage plants, *117*, 118
    profiles, 100
    vegetables, profiles, 140
    See also Groundcovers
Castor bean (*Ricinus communis*)
    profile, 40
    'Sanguineus', *40*
Catharanthus. See Periwinkle
Celosia, plume, 144
Chamomile (*Chamaemelum nobile*), 34, *34*
Change bedding, 18
Cherry, weeping (*Prunus subhirtella* 'Pendula'), 78, *78*
Chervil, 113
Chinese evergreen (*Aglaonema*), 85
Chives (*Allium schoenoprasum*), 113, 114, *114*
Cholla (*Opuntia*), *96*
Chrysalidocarpus lutescens. See Palms: areca
Chrysanthemum (mum), 17, 28, 46, 178, *178*
Citrofortunella microcarpa. See Kumquat
Citrus
    dwarf, profiles, 148
    edible flowers, 122
    growing from seed, *167*
    how to grow, 146–147
Clay soils, identifying, *141*
Clematis (*Clematis*)
    interplanting with roses, *45*
    for shade, 56
    supports for, *64*
    sweet autumn (*C. terniflora*), 64, *65*, *66*, 66
Clivia (*Clivia miniata*), 108, *108*
Cocoa bean hulls, as mulch, 53
Codiaeum. See Croton
Coir liners, for hanging baskets, 153
Cold frames, building, 176–*177*
Cold-weather damage
    to citrus, preventing, 147, 148
    to fall gardens, 17
    frost dates, map, *181*
    overwintering houseplants, 171
    Plant Hardiness map, *180*
    roses, 162, 163
    watering to prevent, 75
Coleus (*Solenostemon*), 12, *13*, 25, 87
    'Limelight', 72
    making cuttings, 178, *178*
    profile, 18
    'Wizard Hybrids', *18*
Color
    for container plantings, *129*, 130
    for dark areas, 68–70
Compost, 79, 141, *163*
Conifers for hot, dry spots, 74

Container plants
    centerpieces, bedding plant, 124–125
    centerpieces, living herb, 112–114
    citrus trees, *146*, 147
    cut flowers, 142–144
    deck transformation, 128–129
    doorstep garden, 12–*13, 15*
    fertilizing, 12, 31, 35
    fragrant, 12, 14
    front porch seasonals, 28–30
    garden room oasis, 54–*55*
    grooming, 12
    growth cycle, *149*
    hanging baskets, *54*, 100, 150–152
    ideal partners, 130
    invasive plants as, 41
    lettuce as, *154*, 155
    mulching, 12, 25
    planting, *12*, *46*, 98, *98*, 131
    potting mixes for, 19, 31, 131
    repotting, 149
    as screens, 38–*39*
    towers, 98–*99*
    tree roses, *160, 161*
    trees as, 46–49
    vegetables as, 136
    watering, 12
    See also Houseplants
Containers (pots)
    as candle-holders, 116–*117*
    choosing, 15
    clay, soaking, 15
    drainage holes, *12*
    as fountains, 76, 77
    for hanging baskets, 150–*151, 153*
    polystyrene urns, 28–29
    for seed-starting, 137
    stabilizing, 25, 28
    utility pots, 12
    for wall garden, 94–95
    wattle, 168, *169*
Coral bells, 90
Cordyline (*Cordyline*)
    C. terminalis 'Lilliput', *26*
    profile, 26
Coreopsis, 51
Cornus. See Dogwood
Cortaderia selloana. See Pampas grass
Crabapple (*Malus*), 'Maypole', 90, *92*
Croton (*Codiaeum*)
    C. variegatum var. *pictum*, *26*
    profile, 26
Cucumber
    'Marketmore', *140*
    profile, 140
Cucurbita pepo. See Gourd, ornamental
Cupflower (*Nierembergia*)
    profile, 126
    'Purple Robe', *126*
Cupressus. See Cypress
Curbside flowers, *16*–17
Cut flowers
    for containers, 142–144
    front porch seasonals, 28–31
    growing bulbs indoors, 106–109

    in kitchen, 82
    staking plants, 145
Cuttings
    easy-to-root plants, profiles, 178
    techniques for making, 178, *179*
Cyclamen (*Cyclamen persicum*)
    as houseplant, 82
    'Miracle', *84*
    profile, 84
    'Sierra', *84*
Cypress (*Cupressus*)
    C. sempervirens 'Stricta, *74*
    profile, 74

D

Daffodil, 17, 46, *47*, 155
Dahlia, growing indoors, 109
Daisy, marguerite, 46, *47*, 72
Daylily 'Happy Returns', 17
Deadheading, 115
Dead nettle (*Lamium maculatum*), 69, 90, *118*
    'Beedham's white, 116
    profiles, 70, 118
    'White Nancy', *70*
Decks, accent planters for, *128*–129
Deschampsia caespitosa. See Tufted hair grass
Dianthus
    'Amazon Neon Cherry', *144*
    dividing, *71*
    profile, 144
Dicentra. See Bleeding heart
Dichondra 'Silver Falls', 118, *118*
Digitalis purpurea. See Foxglove
Dill (*Anethum graveolens*), 62, *62*
Display techniques
    centerpieces, bedding plant, 124–125
    centerpieces, living herb, 112–114
    container towers, 98–*99*
    dish gardens for cacti, *97*
    framing views, 90–*91*
    garden on a wall, 94–95, *97*
    growing bulbs indoors, 106–109
    large container plantings, *128*–129
    orchid window garden, *102*–104
    potting bench as party bar, *120*–121
    sculpture in the garden, *86*–87
    violets in the kitchen, 82–84
    wattle holding beds, 168, *169*
Dogwood, variegated red-twig (*Cornus alba* 'Elegantissima'), 87
Doorstep garden, 12–*13*
Dracaena (*Dracaena*)
    D. marginata 'Tricolor', *26*
    profile, 26
Drainage
    for cacti and succulents, 97
    for indoor plants, 123
    for pots, *12*
    soil selection and, 31
    watering and, 75
Drip-irrigation systems, 63, *63*
Drought stress, impact on houseplants, 84

Drought-tolerant plants
    evergreen trees and shrubs, 74
    supplemental watering for, 75

E

Earthworms, 141
Edging, for lawns, *87*, 89
Entryways
    back door makeover, *24–25*
    curbside flowers, *16*–17
    doorstep garden, 12–15
    front porch seasonals, 28–30
Erosion control, 88
Espaliers, 139
Euonymus fortunei. See Wintercreeper
Euphorbia. See Spurge
Evergreens for hot, dry spots, 74

F

Fan flower (*Scaevola*), 129
    'Blue Wonder', *30*
    profile, 30
Feather reed grass (*Calamagrostis acutiflora*)
    'Karl Foerster', *62*, *72*, 87
    profile, 62
Fences. *See* Screens and fences
Ferns, 56, 61, 77
Fertilizing
    African violets, *82*
    amaryllis, 109
    bedding plants, 18, *127*
    bulbs, 109
    cacti and succulents, *95*
    choosing and applying fertilizers, 35
    citrus, *147*
    container plants, *12,* 31, 35, *131, 144, 149*
    hanging baskets, 150
    indoor plants, 123
    lawns, *35*
    lettuce, *155*
    orchids, 103
    ornamental grasses, 88
    roses, 22
Flowers, edible, 113, 114, 121, *121*, 122
Focal points. *See* Display techniques
Forsythia (*Forsythia intermedia*), 48, *48*
Fortunella margarita. See Calamondin
Fountain grass (*Pennisetum*)
    P. allopecuroides 'Moudry', *88*
    profile, 88
    purple (*P. setaceum*), 129, 130, *130*
Fountains, how to make, 76–77

Foxglove (*Digitalis purpurea*)
    'Foxy', *56*
    profile, 56
Fragrant plants
    bower of flowers, 50–53
    for doorstep gardens, 12, 14
    groundcovers, 33, 34
French intensive gardens, 134, *135*

Front porch screen, 42–45
Front yards
    curbside flowers, *16*–17
    doorstep garden, *12–13, 15*
    front porch seasonals, 28–30
Fruit trees
    columnar, for small spaces, 90, 92
    espaliered, 139
    planting, 93
    See also specific fruit trees
Fuchsia
    profile, 100
    'Swingtime', *100*

G

Garden gate upgrade, *32–33*
Gardenia, 122
Garden room oasis, 54–*55*
Garden rooms, plants for, 170–171
Gates, upgrading, 32–33
Gayfeather (*Liatris*), *29*
Geranium (*Pelargonium*)
    balcony (*P. peltatum*), 100, *100*
    fancy-leaved, 12, *13*
    making cuttings, 179, *179*
    pots for, 15
    profile, 18
    P. x *hortorum* 'Orbit Hot Pink', *18*
    rose, 12, *13*
    scented, 12, *13*, 179
Ghost plant (*Graptopetalum paraguayense*), *94*, 95, 96, *96*
Ginger, edible flowers, 122
Gloxinia (*Sinningia speciosa*), 84, *84*
Gourd, ornamental (*Cucurbita pepo*), 66, *66*
Grapefruit, tips on growing, 147
Grape (*Vitis vinifera*), 44, *44*
Graptopetalum paraguayense. See Ghost plant
Grasses, ornamental, 17, *29*
    design role, 51
    grooming, *51*
    light-colored, *68*, 69
    peek-a-boo, 62
    profiles, 88
    as screens, 72
    for water gardens, 77, 78
    See also specific grasses
Gravel, as mulch, *12*, 53, *79*
Grooming
    amaryllis, 106
    citrus, 147
    container plants, 12
    to control invasive plants, 41
    deadheading, 115
    herbal groundcovers, 34
    indoor plants, 123, 171
    orchids, 105
    ornamental grasses, 88
    roses, 20, 162
    Russian sage, *51*
    vines, *64*, 67

Groundcovers
    bottle-glass mat, *32–33*
    design role, 51
    edging for, *87*, 89
    fragrant, profiles, 34
    invasive, 41
    See also specific groundcover plants
Gysophila paniculata. See Baby's breath

H

Hakone grass, Japanese (*Hakonechloa macra*), 69
    'Aureola', 77, *77*, *78*
    profile, 78
Hand watering, 63, *63*
Hanging baskets
    caring for, 152
    herbs for, 150–152
    misters for, *54*
    planting, coir liners, 153, *153*
    planting, sphagnum moss, *150*
    plants for, profiles, 100
Haworthia, 96
Heat
    impact on houseplants, 84
    protecting transplants from, 119
    watering and, 75
Hedges
    bamboo, no-dig, 38–*39*
    fast-growing plants, 40
    flowering, 50–53
Helichrysum bracteatum. See Strawflower
Helichrysum petiolare. See Licorice plant
Helictotrichon sempervirens. See Blue oat grass
Heliopsis. See Sunflower, false
Heliotrope (*Heliotropium*), 14, *14*
Helleborus niger. See Lenten rose
Hen and chicks (*Sempervivum*), 95
Herbicides, types of, 27
Herbs
    gravel mulches for, 79
    as groundcovers, 33, 34
    for hanging baskets, 150–152
    living herb centerpieces, 112–114
    pots for, 15
    profiles, 114
Hibiscus, Chinese (*Hibiscus rosa-sinensis*), 48, *48*, 122
Hoeing, to control weeds, *27*
Honeydew, identifying, *101*
Honeysuckle, 54, *55*, 64, *65*
Hops vine, golden (*Humulus lupulus* 'Aureus'), 20, 66, *66*
Hose-end sprayers, 35

Hosta (*Hosta*), 61, 69
    gold-leaved, 168
    H. fortunei 'Gold Standard', *70*
    profile, 70
    for shade, 56
    variegated, 77

Houseplants
cacti and succulents as, 95
cut flowers indoors, 106–109
easy flowering, 84
indoor-outdoor, profiles, 170
light for, 82, 85
orchids, 102–105
overwintering, 171
tips on growing, 123
violets in the kitchen, 82–84
See also specific houseplants
Humidity
for African violets, 82
for citrus plants, 147
for orchids, *102, 103,* 104
Humulus lupulus 'Aureus'. *See* Hops vine, golden
Hyacinth, Dutch (*Hyacinthus orientalis*), 46, *47, 108*
'Blue Jacket', 14, *14*
profile, 108
Hyacinth, grape (*Muscari*), 17
Hyacinth bean (*Lablab purpureus*), 66, *66*
Hydrangea (*Hydrangea*), 28, *28*
'Annabelle', 64, *65*
climbing (*H. petiolaris*), 44, *44,* 67
H. macrocarpa 'Kluis Superba', *170*
profile, 170
for shade, 56
Hypericum. See St. Johnswort

I

Impatiens (*Impatiens*), 168
New Guinea (*I. hawkeri*), 130
New Guinea (*I. hawkeri*) 'Celebretta Purple', *130*
profile, 18
'Super Elfin hybrids', *18, 131*
Imperata cylindrica. See Japanese blood grass
Indoor plants. *See* Houseplants
Insecticides, reading labels, *175*
Insect pests
of citrus plants, 147
diagnosing, 101, *149*
of houseplants, 171, *171*
Invasive plants. *See* Weeds
Ipomoea batatas. See Sweet potato
Ipomoea tricolor. See Morning glory
Iris (*Iris*)
dividing, *71*
Siberian (*I. sibirica*), 78
Siberian (*I. sibirica*) 'Marcus Perry', *78*
Irrigation systems. *See* Watering
Ivy, Boston, 67
Ivy, English, 12, *13,* 41
making cuttings, 178, *178*
supports for, *45*
variegated, *90*
Ixora. See Jungle flame

J

Jade plant, 96
Japanese blood grass (*Imperata cylindrica*)
profile, 88
'Red Baron', *88*
Japanese gardens, screens for, *72*
Jasmine (*Jasminum*), 54, *55*
Confederate, *154,* 155
edible flowers, 122
J. polyanthum, 170, *170*
'Maid of Orleans', 12, *13*
Johnny-jump-up (*Viola tricolor*), 18, 46, *47,* 114, *114*
Jungle flame (*Ixora*), 168
I. longifolia, 170
profile, 170
Juniper (*Juniperus*), 74
'Medora', *72, 73*
profile, 74

K

Kalanchoe (*Kalanchoe blossfeldiana*), 54
'Maxi Neon Rose', *84*
profile, 84
Kale, ornamental (*Brassica oleracea*), 17
'Chidora Red', *30*
profile, 30
Kitchen plants
from pits and seeds, 167
profiles, 166
See also Herbs; Vegetables
Knots, to lash poles, *43*
Kumquat (x *Citrofortunella microcarpa*), *148*
profile, 148
tips on growing, 147

L

Lablab purpureus. See Hyacinth bean
Lamium. *See* Dead nettle
Landscape cloth, *25*
Larkspur
as cut flower, 144
direct-sowing, 157
Laurus nobilis. See Bay, sweet
Lavender, 46, 113
Lawn
edging for, *87, 89*
fertilizing, *35*
removing, 25
Lemon balm, 41
Lemon (*Citrus*)
Meyer (*C. limon* 'Meyer Improved'), 148, *148*
tips on growing, 147
Lemongrass, profile, 166
Lemon verbena (*Aloysia triphylla*), 46, 130, *130*
Lenten rose (*Helleborus niger*), 41
Lettuce
'Buttercrunch', *156*
in containers, *154,* 155
'Deer Tongue', *156*

profiles, 156
'Red Fire', *156*
'Royal Oak Leaf', *156*
speckled 'Bunte Forellenschluss', *156*
Liatris. See Gayfeather
Licorice, lemon, 72
Licorice plant (*Helichrysum petiolare*), 129
profile, 118
'Rondello', *118*
Lighting
for cacti and succulents, 97
for citrus plants, 147
for houseplants, 82, 85
for orchids, 103, 104
for seed-starting, *137*
Lilac, Korean, 90
Lily (*Lilium*), 29
Easter (*L. longiflorum*), 84, 108, *108*
for shade, 56
'Stargazer' oriental, 14, *14,* 168
Lime (*Citrus*)
Mexican or Key (*C. aurantifolia*), 148, *148*
tips on growing, 147
Lithops, 96
Loam soils, identifying, *141*
Lobelia (*Lobelia*), 12, *13,* 78, 116
Loosestrife (*Lysimachia*)
L. clethroides, 40
profile, 40
as weed, *41*
Lythrum, 41

M

Macleaya microcarpa. See Plume poppy
Maiden grass (*Miscanthus sinensis*)
profile, 88
'Rotsilber', *88*
Malus. See Apple; Crabapple
Mammillaria (*Mammillaria*)
M. elongata 'Irish Red', *96*
profile, 96
Mandevilla (*Mandevilla sanderi*)
profile, 44
'Red Riding Hood', *44*
Mango
growing from seed, *167*
profile, 166
Manure, benefits, 141
Maple, flowering (*Abutilon*)
profile, 48
'Vesuvius Red', *48*
Maple, Japanese (*Acer palmatum*)
Dissectum, *52*
profile, 52
for shade, 56
Marigold (*Tagetes*)
African (*T. erecta*), 144, *144*
dwarf or French (*T. patula*), *124,* 126, *126*
edible flowers, 113
Marjoram (*Origanum onites*), 113, 150
'Aureum', *152*
profile, 152

Meadow rue, lavender mist (*Thalictrum rochebrunianum* 'Lavender Mist'), 62, *62*
Mealybugs
    on citrus plants, 147
    on houseplants, *171*
    identifying, *101*
Metric conversion chart, 180
Mint (*Mentha*)
    Corsican (*M. requienii*), 34, *34*
    M. spicata, *40*
    orange, 113
    peppermint, 113
    pineapple (*M. suaveolens*), 150, 152
    pineapple (*M. suaveolens*) 'Variegata', *152*
    profile, 40
Mirrors, design role, *60*–61
Miscanthus sinensis. See Maiden grass
Misters, for garden room oasis, 54–*55*
Mondo grass, black (*Ophiopogon planiscapis* 'Nigriscens'), 88, *88*
Morning glory (*Ipomoea tricolor*)
    'Mt. Fuji Hybrids', *66*
    profile, 66
Mulch
    about, 53, 79
    to conserve moisture, 75
    to control weeds, *24*, 27
    light-colored, 69
    for pot surfaces, 12, 25
    to prevent cold-weather damage, 163
Muscari. See Hyacinth, grape

N

Narcissus (paper-white), 108, *108*
Nasturtium (*Tropaeolum majus*), 122, *122*
Nemesia (*Nemesia strumosa*), 126, *126*
Neoregelia carolinea meyendorfii 'Albomarginata', *170*
Net vine supports, *64*
Nierembergia. See Cupflower

O

Ocimum basilicum. See Basil
Onion, pearl
    'Crystal Wax', *136*
    profile, 136
Ophiopogon planiscapis 'Nigriscens'. *See* Mondo grass, black
Opuntia. See Bunny ears; Cholla; Prickly pear
Orange, dwarf (*Fortunella margarita*)
    'Nagami', *148*
    profile, 148
Orange, tips on growing, 147
Orchids, *102*
    caring for, 103, 104, *105*
    lighting for, *85*
    Phragmipedium, 103
    pots for, 15
    profiles of easiest, 104
    repotting, *105*

Orchids, cymbidium (*Cymbidium ultimatum*)
    profile, 104
    'Santa Barbara', *104*
Orchids, dancing lady (*Oncidium*), 103
    'Kathleen', *104*
    profile, 104
Orchids, dendrobium (*Dendrobium*)
    'Emerald Fantasy', 103
    'Orchid Acres Stephanie', *104*
    profile, 104
Orchids, moth (*Phalaenopsis*), 103
    grooming, *105*
    'KB's Happy Camper', *104*
    profile, 104
Orchids, pansy (*Miltonia* or *Miltonipsis*)
    'Maurice Powers', *104*
    profile, 104
Orchid window garden, *102*–103
Oregano (*Origanum vulgare*), 113
    'Aureum', 34, *34*
Origanum onites. See Marjoram
Ortho Home Gardeners' Problem Solver, 101

P

Pachysandra, 77
Palms
    areca (*Chrysalidocarpus lutescens*), 26, *26*
    in containers, 25
Pampas grass (*Cortaderia selloana*), 40, *40*
Pansy (*Viola*)
    edible flowers, 113
    to hide bulbs, 17
    Johnny-jump-up (*V. tricolor*), 18, 46, *47*, 114, *114*
    profile, 18
    P. x *wittrockiana* 'Universal Plus', *18*
Parsley (*Petroselinum crispum*), 113
    'Broad Leaf Italian', 152, *152*
Party ideas
    bedding plant centerpieces, 124–*125*
    birdbath candle-holder, 116–*117*
    deck transformation, *128*–129
    living herb centerpieces, *112*–113
    potting bench as party bar, *120*–121
    wattle holding beds, 168, *169*
Passionflower (*Passiflora* x *belotii*)
    'Imperatrice Eugenie', *122*
    profile, 122
Paving materials
    bottle-glass mat, *32*–33
    mulches for, 53
Peace lily (*Spathiphyllum*), 85, *85*
Peas
    profile, 140
    'Super Sugar Snap Improved', *140*
Peek-a-boo plants, 61, 62
Pelargonium. See Geranium
Pennisetum. See Fountain grass
Penola, *131*
Penta, 72, 168

Peppers, 54, *138*, 139
    'Lipstick', *136*
    profile, 136
Perennial plants, dividing, *71*
Pergolas, 45, *45*
Periwinkle (*Catharanthus*), 54, 72
Periwinkle (*Vinca*), 90
    V. major and minor, 70
    V. major 'Variegata', *70*
Perovskia atriplicifolia. See Sage, Russian
Peruvian daffodil, growing indoors, 109
Peruvian old man, 96
Pest control, diagnosing problems, 101, 149, 171
Pesticides, reading labels, *175*
Petroselinum crispum. See Parsley
Petunia, *13*, 54, 72, 129
    'Hulahoop Hybrids', *18*
    mini, 12
    profile, 18
    'Purple Wave', *15*
Philodendron (*Philodendron*), 54, *55*
    lighting for, *85*
    profile, 26
    'Xanadu', *26*
Picea. See Spruce
Pineapple
    growing from seed, 167
    profile, 166
Pine (*Pinus*)
    P. mugo 'Kobold', *74*
    profile, 74
Pine straw, as mulch, 53
Plant diseases, diagnosing, 101, *149*
Planting and transplanting
    bare-root roses, *23*
    bedding plants, 127
    bulbs in containers, 109
    cacti and succulents, 97
    container gardens, *12*, 46, 98, *98*, *131*
    garden on a wall, *95*
    hanging baskets, 150, *153*
    palms in containers, 25
    raised beds, *17*
    repotting container plants, *149*
    repotting houseplants, 123
    repotting orchids, *105*
    space requirements, 127, *127*
    sun and wind protection, 119
    trees and shrubs, 93
    trees and shrubs in containers, 49
    watering after, 75
Planting beds, edging for, 87, 89
Planting pockets, in containers, *46*
Plant problems, diagnosing, 101, *149*
Plants
    fast-growing, 40
    moisture requirements, 75
    peek-a-boo, 61, 62
    protecting during construction, *69*
Plectranthus (*Plectranthus*)
    P. argentatus, 30
    profile, 30
    purple (*P. hillardiae*), 168, 170, *170*

Plumbago, 54, *55*
Plume poppy (*Macleaya microcarpa*)
    'Kalway's Coral Plume', *52*
    profile, 52
Poisonous flowers, 122
Pollinating citrus, *147*
Polygonum aubertii. See Silver lace vine
Pomegranate, growing from seed, 167
Poppy, direct-sowing, 157
Potagers, 134, *135*
Pots. *See* Containers
Potting benches
    dressing up, *172–173*
    as party bars, *120–121*
    tools and supplies for, 174
Potting mixes
    for African violets, *82*
    for cacti and succulents, 97
    for container plants, *19, 31, 131*
    for seed-starting, *137*
Prickly pear (*Opuntia*), 96, *96*
Primrose (*Primula vulgaris*)
    'Pageant Hybrids', *56*
    profile, 56
Propagating plants
    dividing perennials, *71*
    easy-to-root plants, profiles, 178
    ornamental grasses, 88
Pruning
    climbing roses, 20, 22
    to control invasive plants, 41
    to control vines, 66, 67
Prunus subhirtella 'Pendula'. *See* Cherry,
    weeping
Pussy willow, tree-form
    standards, 46, *47*

Q

Quarantining plants, *171*

R

Rain barrels, *63*
Raised beds
    curbside flowers, *16–17*
    no-dig, building, 19
    small-space vegetable gardens,
        134–135
    soils for, 19
Ramadas, 54, *55*
Resources, plants and supplies, 182???
Ricinus communis. See Castor bean
Rosemary (*Rosmarinus officinalis*), 113
    profile, 118
    'Prostratus', *118*
Rose of Sharon, edible flowers, 122
Rose (*Rosa*)
    arbors for, 20–23
    bare root, buying and planting, 23
    'Flower Carpet', 78, *78*, 90, *90*
    'Ingrid Bergman', 14, *14*
    interplanting with clematis, 45
    preparing for winter, 163

as screens, 64
Rose (*Rosa*), climbing
    'Blaze Improved', 22, *22*
    'John Cabot', 20, *20, 21,* 22, *22*
    Lady Banks, 22, *22*
    'Madame Alfred Carriere', 22, *22*
    'New Dawn', 20, *21,* 22, *22*
    supports for, *45*
    training and pruning, 20
Rose (*Rosa*), trees, 90, 160, *161*
    'Black Jade', 162, *162*
    'Bonica', 162, *162*
    'Graham Thomas', 162, *162*
    'Knock Out', 162, *162*
    'Mister Lincoln', *48*
    preparing for winter, 162, 163
    profiles, 48, 162
    'Starry Night', 162, *162*
Row covers, floating, 119

S

Sage, Russian (*Perovskia atriplicifolia*), *50,*
   51, 52
    grooming, *51*
    profile, 52
Sage (*Salvia*), 113
    annual (*S. coccinea*), 126
    annual (*S. farinacea* 'Rhea'), *126*
    annual (*S. splendens*), 126
    annual (*S. splendens* 'Hot Shot'), *126*
    blue, 72, 144
    'Lady in Red', 54
    pineapple (*S. elegans*), 122, *122*
Sandy soils, identifying, *141*
Savory, 113
Scaevola. See Fan flower
Scale insects
    on citrus plants, 147
    on houseplants, *171*
    identifying, *101*
Scarlet runner bean, 66
Schlumbergera bridgesii. See Cactus:
  holiday
Screens and fences
    flowering, *50–53*
    for front porch privacy, *42–43*
    growing vines on, 45
    to hide air conditioners, 72, *73*
    lattice, *68, 69*
    no-dig hedge, *38–39*
    peek-a-boo plants, 61, 62
    for seedling protection, 119
    trellised tomatoes as, *138–139*
    vines as, 64–66
    wattle, 168
Sculpture
    benches as, *50,* 51
    display techniques, *86–87*
Seasonal interest
    container plants, 46, 47, 131
    curbside flowers, *16–17*
    for front porch, 28–30
    houseplants for, 84

lettuces for every season, 156
    vegetables for, 134
Sedge, drooping (*Carex pendula*), 78, *78*
Sedum (*Sedum*)
    burro's tail (*S. morganianum*), *94, 95,*
        96, *96*
    pork and beans, 95
Seedlings
    sun and wind protection, 119
    thinning, *142, 155, 157*
Seed sowing
    citrus seeds, 147, *147*
    in containers, 142, *142,* 144
    direct-sowing, *157*
    kitchen plants, 166–167
    lettuce, *155,* 156
    starting indoors, 137
Sempervivum. See Hen and chicks
Shade
    to protect lettuce, *154,* 155
    to protect seedlings, 119
    ramadas for, 54, *55*
Shade and sun patterns, 57, 70
Shade plants
    garden room oasis, 54–55
    light-colored, 68–70
    profiles, 56
    See also specific shade plants
Shovel-pruning, 41
Shrubs
    in containers, *49, 154,* 155
    for hot, dry spots, 74
    planting, 93
    tree-form standards, 46, 47, 48
Silver lace vine (*Polygonum aubertii*), 52,
   52, 66
Sinningia speciosa. See Gloxinia
Small gardens
    container towers, 98–*99*
    overcoming limitations of, 60–62
    vegetable beds for, 134–136
Snapdragon (*Antirrhinum*), *29*
    'Luminare', *100*
    'Rocket Golden', 72
    'Rocket Hybrid', 144, *144*
    trailing, 100
Soaker hoses, *63*
Soil amendments, 31, 78, 141
Soil preparation, for bedding plants, 127
Soils. *See* Potting mixes
Soil types, assessing, 141, *141*
Solenostemon. See Coleus
Spathiphyllum. See Peace lily
Sphagnum moss, *150*
Spider mites
    on citrus plants, 147
    on houseplants, *171*
    identifying, *101*
Spinach, Malabar or Indian, 140, *140*
Sprinkler systems, about, 63
Spruce (*Picea*), 74, *74*
Spurge (*Euphorbia*)
    E. characias wulfenii, 56
    profile, 56

Staking
    flowering plants, 145
    trees, pros and cons, 93
Stevia, *112*
St. Johnswort, tricolored (*Hypericum* x *moseranum* 'Tricolor'), 118, *118*
Stock, as cut flower, 144
Storage areas
    for garden tools, 160–*161*
    in potting benches, 174
    screens to hide, 38, 64, *65*
Strauss, Peter, 6–7
Strawflower (*Helichrysum bracteatum*), 129
    'Bright Bikinis', *130*
    profile, 130
String-of-beads plant, 96
Succulents. *See* Cacti and succulents
Sunflower, false (*Heliopsis*), 87
Supports for plants. *See* Arbors; Staking; Trellises
Sweet alyssum, 46, 47
Sweet flag, 78
Sweet pea, 45
Sweet potato (*Ipomoea batatas*)
    'Blackie', *44*
    'Marguerite', 129
    profile, 44, 166
    'Terrace Lime', *44*
    'Tricolor', *44*
Sweet vernal grass (*Anthoxanthum odoratum*), 113, 114, *114*

T

Tagetes. See Marigold
Tangerine, clementine (Citrus reticulata 'Clementine')★★★, 148, *148*
Taxus cuspidata. See Yew, Japanese
Thalictrum. See Meadow rue
Thuja. See Arborvitae
Thyme, creeping (*Thymus*), 33, *152*
    golden, 33
    profile, 34
    'Victor Reiter', *34*
Thyme, English or French (*Thymus vulgaris*)
    profile, 152
    'Silver Posie', *152*
Tilling, about, *141*
Tobacco, flowering (*Nicotiana sylvestris*)
    candlestick, 14, *14*
    as cut flower, 144
Tomato
    'Big Beef', *140*
    heirloom, *138*
    indeterminate, *138*, 139, 140
    'Minibel', *136*
    profile, 136
    trellised, as screens, *138–139*
Tools
    for potting bench, 174
    storing, 160–161

Trees
    in containers, 46–49, 155
    for hot, dry spots, 74
    mulching, *79*
    planting, *93*
    shade patterns, 56, 57
    shrubs trained as, 46–48
    staking, 93
    See also Citrus; Fruit trees; *specific trees*
Trellises
    bamboo, *42–43*
    selecting the right support, 44, 45, 64, 67
    for vegetable gardens, 136, *138–139*, 140, *154*
Tropaeolum majus. See Nasturtium
Tropical plants
    for garden room oasis, 54
    growing outdoors, 26
    See also Houseplants
Trumpet vine, 66
Tufted hair grass (*Deschampsia caespitosa*)
    'Goldschleier', *88*
    profile, 88
Tulip, 17

U

USDA Plant Hardiness map, *180*

V

Variegated plants, 68–70
Vegetable gardens, small-space, 134–136
Vegetables
    climbing, profiles, 140
    compact varieties, profiles, 136
    starting seeds indoors, *137*
    trellised tomato screens, *138–139*
Verbena
    'Silver Anne', *100*
    trailing, 100
Views, framing, 90–*91*
Vines
    climbing vegetables, 140
    controlling, *64*, 66, 67
    to disguise and distract, 64–67
    fast-growing, 66
    for front porch privacy, *42–45*
    supports for, 44, 45, 64, 67
    See also specific vining plants
Viola. See Pansy
Viola tricolor. See Johnny-jump-up
Violets in the kitchen, 82–84
Virginia creeper, 43, 67
Visual illusions
    light in dark areas, *68–70*
    mirrors to create, *60–61*
    peek-a-boo plants, 61, 62
    screening with vines, 64–67
    small spaces appear bigger, *60–61*
Vitis vinifera. See Grape

W

Wall gardens, *94–95*, *97*
Walls, light-colored, 69
Water conservation techniques, 63
Water gardens, 76–78
Watering
    amaryllis, 106
    bedding plants, 18, 127
    cacti and succulents, 95, 97
    citrus, 147
    container plants, 12, *131*, 144, *149*
    hanging baskets, 150, 152
    herbal groundcovers, 34
    indoor plants, 123
    misters, 54–*55*
    orchids, 103, *103*
    ornamental grasses, 88
    roses, 22, 162
    seedlings, indoors, *137*
    techniques and timing, 63, 75
Wattle holding beds, 168, *169*
Weed control
    in groundcovers, 34
    herbicides, 27
    landscape cloth, *25*
    mechanical methods, 27, 40
    mulching, *24*, 27
Weeds
    bamboo as, 38
    containing, 41
    definition, 27
    groundcovers as, 41
Wind, protecting transplants from, 119
Wintercreeper (*Euonymus fortunei*)
    'Emerald 'n' Gold', *70*
    profile, 70
Wisteria
    controlling, 66, *67*
    supports for, 45, *45*
Wood chips, as mulch, 53

Y

Yarrow, wooly (*Achillea tomentosa*)
    'Aurea', *34*
    profile, 34
Yew, Japanese (*Taxus cuspidata*)
    'Dwarf Bright', *70*
    profile, 70
Yucca (*Yucca filamentosa*), 122, *122*

Z

Zantedeschia rehmannii violacea. See Calla lily
Zinnia (*Zinnia elegans*)
    'Bouquet', *144*
    for cut flowers, 142, *142*, *143*
    profile, 144

Index of Featured Plants

FLOWERS: ANNUALS, PERENNIALS,
ROSES, BULBS

14   Fragrance for Containers
18   Bedding Plant All Stars
22   Great Climbing Roses
30   Seasonal Drop-Ins for Container Gardens
56   Shade-Lovers
62   Peek-A-Boo Plants
100 Cascading, Spilling Flowers
118 Cascading Foliage Plants
126 Bedding All-Stars for Summer-Long Color
130 Ideal Container Partners
144 Cut Flowers for Containers
162 Favorite Tree Roses

LANDSCAPE PLANTS: TREES, SHRUBS, VINES,
GROUNDCOVERS, FERNS, GRASSES

34   Fragrance Underfoot
40   Fast-Growing Plants
44   Good Vines for Different Supports
48   Standard Shrubs and Small Trees
52   Lacy Backdrops
66   Fast-Growing Vines
70   Light-Colored Shade-Lovers
74   Evergreens for Hot, Dry Spots
78   For a Waterside Effect
88   Ornamental Grasses
178 Plants Easy to Root from Cuttings

108

EDIBLES: VEGETABLES, FRUITS, HERBS

92   Columnar Fruit Trees for Small Spaces
114 Ornamental Edibles for Small Containers
122 Edible Tropical Flowers
136 Small-Space Vegetables
140 Vegetables That Climb
148 Best Dwarf Citrus
152 Kitchen Herbs for Hanging Baskets
156 Lettuce for Every Season

HOUSEPLANTS

26   Tropicals Outdoors
84   Easy Flowering Houseplants
96   Favorite Cacti and Succulents
104 Easiest Orchids
108 Favorite Bulbs for Indoor Blooms
166 Kitchen Plants
170 Colorful Indoor-Outdoor Plants

34

14

Index of Techniques

SOILS AND PLANTING
19 Making a No-Dig Bed
23 Planting a Bare-Root Rose
93 Planting a Tree or Shrub
127 Planting Bedding Plants
141 Improving Soil

CLIMATE
57 Understanding Shade and Sun
85 Providing the Right Light Indoors
119 Protecting Transplants from Sun and Wind
163 Preparing Roses for Winter
171 Bringing Houseplants Indoors for the Winter

WINTER MULCHING, WEED CONTROL, PEST CONTROL

27 Preventing Weeds
41 Containing Invasive Plants
53 Recommended Mulches
79 Mulching
101 Catching Plant Problems Early
175 Reading Pest Control Labels

WATERING, FEEDING

35 Choosing and Applying Plant Food
63 Watering
75 Deciding When to Water
97 Caring for Cacti and Succulents

PRUNING, GROOMING, TRAINING
45 Providing the Right Support for the Vine
67 Controlling Vines
89 Edging Between Lawn and Beds
115 Grooming and Deadheading
145 Staking Flowers

PROPAGATION
71 Dividing Perennials
137 Starting Plants from Seed Indoors
157 Direct-Sowing Seeds
167 Plants from Pits and Seeds
179 Making a Cutting

CONTAINER GARDENING
15 Choosing the Right Pot
31 Choosing the Right Soil for Containers
49 Growing Trees and Shrubs in Containers
105 Repotting Orchids
109 Planting and Growing Tender Bulbs in a Container
123 Growing Indoor Plants
131 Planting in Big Containers
149 Repotting a Container Plant
153 Planting Hanging Baskets with Coir Liner

Beautiful Gardens Made Easy

Executive Editor, Gardening: Michael McKinley
Writers: Elvin McDonald, Peter Strauss
Technical Editors for The Scotts Company: Keith Baeder, Bonny Beetham, Scott Hanley, Rich Foster, and the entire Miracle-Gro® Marketing and Research & Development teams
Design Director: Mary Pat Crowley, Crowley Design, LLC
Production Designer and Stylist: Wade Scherrer
Photographers: Marty Baldwin, Scott Little, Blaine Moats, Jay Wilde
Contributing Illustrator: Michael Burns
Assistant Editor: Harijs Priekulis
Copy Chief: Terri Fredrickson
Copy and Production Editor: Victoria Forlini
Editorial Operations Manager: Karen Schirm
Managers, Book Production: Pam Kvitne, Marjorie J. Schenkelberg, Rick von Holdt
Contributing Copy Editor: Kim Catanzarite
Contributing Technical Proofreader: Barbara Feller-Roth
Contributing Proofreaders: Susan Brown, Barbara J. Stokes
Indexer: Ellen Davenport
Editorial and Design Assistants: Kathleen Stevens, Karen McFadden
Contributing Map Illustrator: Jana Fothergill

Meredith® Books

Editor in Chief: Linda Raglan Cunningham
Design Director: Matt Strelecki
Executive Editor, Gardening and Home Improvement: Benjamin W. Allen

Publisher: James D. Blume
Executive Director, Marketing: Jeffrey Myers
Executive Director, New Business Development: Todd M. Davis
Executive Director, Sales: Ken Zagor
Director, Operations: George A. Susral
Director, Production: Douglas M. Johnston
Business Director: Jim Leonard

Vice President and General Manager: Douglas J. Guendel

Meredith Publishing Group

President, Publishing Group: Stephen M. Lacy
Vice President-Publishing Director: Bob Mate

Meredith Corporation

Chairman and Chief Executive Officer: William T. Kerr

In Memoriam: E.T. Meredith III (1933-2003)

All of us at Meredith® Books are dedicated to providing you with the information and ideas you need to enhance your home and garden. We welcome your comments and suggestions about this book. Write to us at:
Meredith Gardening Books
1716 Locust St.
Des Moines, IA 50309–3023

If you would like to purchase any of our gardening, home improvement, cooking, crafts, or home decorating and design books, check wherever quality books are sold. Or visit us at: meredithbooks.com

If you would like more information on other Miracle-Gro products, call 888-295-6902 or visit us at: www.miraclegro.com

Thanks to

Janet Anderson, Dan Bell, Dawn Bentley, Rachel Brooks, Jo Campney, Ellen deLathouder, William & Mary Dunbar, Jim Egan, Alexander Ervanian, Stephen Exel, Phillis Fitzpatrick, Mary Foust, Kate Carter Frederick, Katy Gammack, Jennie Groves, John Hallstrom, Khanh Hamilton, Randy Hamilton, Tod Hansen, Ginny Haviland, Dan Hickey, Rosie Hollingshead, Anthony Horvath, Bruce Hughes, C. Warner Jackson, Clarence Lamoureux, Josh Landis, Nita Larson, Tex & Randa LeJune, Monica Mayfield, Kathy & Scott McFarlin, Mary Noss Reavely, Bob Reynolds, Brad & Sundie Ruppert, Victoria Scherrer, Vern Schmitt, Jennifer Stodden, Sue Terry, Amy Underwood, Larry Waller, John & Pat Work, John & Adele Zieser

Photographers

(Photographers credited may retain copyright © to the listed photographs.)
L = Left, R = Right, C = Center, B = Bottom, T = Top

William D. Adams: 118TR; **Greg Allikas:** 104; **Ball Seed:** 100BC, 118BC; **Mark Bolton/Garden Picture Library:** 122TR; **Patricia Bruno/Postive Images:** 48TL; **Kim Cornelison:** 12T, 12C, 13, 102, 103, 105, 106TL; **Derek Fell:** 2, 22TR, 22BR, 30TL, 30BC, 44BR, 52BL 52BC, 62BC, 62BR, 66BR, 78BC, 78BR, 84BR, 114BR, 136BL, 136BR, 140BR, 144TL, 144TR, 148BR, 166BL; **John Glover:** 18TL, 26TR, 40TL, 45TL, 45TC, 45BL, 52BR, 56BL, 74BL, 78TL, 148BL, 158, 159R, 170BL, 170BR; **John Glover/Garden Picture Library:** 88BC; **Jerry Harpur:** 34BL, 44TR, 44BL, 66BC, 10TR, 100BC, 130TL; **Doug Hetherington:** 4BL, 11L, 20, 21, 23BR, 27TL, 27BL, 27BR, 35TL, 35TRC, 35BR, 41, 53, 57BR, 63CR, 64, 68, 69, 71TL, 71TR, 71CL, 71C, 71BL, 71BR, 72B, 75TL, 75TC, 75B, 79T, 79B, 89, 101BL, 115L, 115CT, 115CL, 119TL, 119BL, 119BR, 123BL, 124B, 134, 135inset, 141L, 145TL, 145TC, 145TR, 153BR, 155C, 155B, 157TL, 157TC, 157TR, 157BL, 157BC, 166BR, 171TC, 178BC; **Neil Holmes/Garden Picture Library:** 40BC, 122BR, 152BR; **Saxon Holt:** 148TL; **Michael Howes/Garden Picture Library:** 136TL; **Michael Landis:** 149; **Andrew Lawson:** 48BL, 48BC, 52TL, 88TL, 130BL, 162TR, 166BC, 170TR; **Janet Loughrey:** 11R, 22TL, 56BR; **Elvin McDonald:** 145BR; **Scott R. Millard/Ironwood Press:** 54, 55; **Maggie Oster:** 45BR; **Jerry Pavia:** 26TL, 26BR, 34TL, 70BC, 130BC, 170TL, 190C; **Emma Peios/Garden Picture Library:** 148TR; **Diane A. Pratt/Positive Images:** 140BL; **Ann Reilly/Positive Images:** 114TR; **Howard Rice/Positive Images:** 26BL, 162BL; **Richard Shiell:** 3R, 10, 18TR, 18BL, 18BC, 18BR, 22BC, 26BC, 30TR, 30BR, 34BR, 37R, 40TR, 44TL, 44BC, 48TR, 48BR, 52TR, 56BC, 62BL, 74TL, 74TR, 74BC, 74BR, 84TR, 84BL, 108BL, 118TL, 118BR, 126BC, 144BL, 144BC, 144BR, 148inset, 162TL, 170BC; **Stark Bro's Nurseries & Orchards Co.:** 92; **Friedrich Strauss/Garden Picture Library:** 84TL, 118BL; **The Scotts Company:** 6, 7, 15BR, 19B, 71CR, 85BR, 97BR, 115B, 157BR, 163C, 179BR; **Michael S. Thompson:** 22BL, 30BL, 34TR, 34BC, 40BL, 40BR, 56TL, 56TR, 62TL, 62TR, 66TL, 66TR, 66BL, 67BR, 70TL, 70TR, 70BL, 70BR, 78BL, 84BC, 88TR, 88BL, 88BR, 96, 100TL, 100BL, 108TL, 108TR, 108BC, 108BR, 114TL, 114BL, 114BC, 122TL, 122BL, 122BC, 126TL, 126TR, 126BL, 126BR, 130TR, 130BR, 136TR, 136BC, 140TL, 140TR, 140inset, 140BC, 147T, 148BC, 152TL, 152TR, 152BL, 152BC, 156, 162BC, 162BR, 190T; **Rick Wetherbee:** 78TR

On the cover, clockwise from top left: *Zinnia* 'Bouquet' (see page 143); *Calibrachoa* 'Trailing Cherry Pink' and 'Trailing Blue' in stacked pots (see page 99); planting paperwhite narcissus in pots (see page 109); planting seasonal color in "planting pockets" (see page 46).

Note to the Readers: Due to differing conditions, tools, and individual skills, Meredith Corporation assumes no responsibility for any damages, injuries suffered, or losses incurred as a result of following the information published in this book. Before beginning any project, review the instructions carefully, and if any doubts or questions remain, consult local experts or authorities. Because codes and regulations vary greatly, you always should check with authorities to ensure that your project complies with all applicable local codes and regulations. Always read and observe all of the safety precautions provided by manufacturers of any tools, equipment, or supplies, and follow all accepted safety procedures.